DATE DUE

FORENSIC SCIENCE

FROM FIBERS TO FINGERPRINTS

Lisa Yount

CHELSEA HOUSE
PUBLISHERS
An imprint of Infobase Publishing

In memory of my mother,
who taught me to love mystery stories.

FORENSIC SCIENCE: From Fibers to Fingerprints

Copyright © 2007 by Lisa Yount

All rights reserved. No part of this book may be reproduced or utilized in any form or by any means, electronic or mechanical, including photocopying, recording, or by any information storage or retrieval systems, without permission in writing from the publisher. For information contact:

Chelsea House
An imprint of Infobase Publishing
132 West 31st Street
New York NY 10001

Library of Congress Cataloging-in-Publication Data
Yount, Lisa.
　　Forensic science: from fibers to fingerprints / Lisa Yount.
　　　　p. cm. — (Milestones in discovery and invention)
　　Includes bibliographical references and index.
　　ISBN 0-8160-5751-6
　　1. Forensic sciences—History—Juvenile literature. 2. Forensic scientists—Juvenile literature. 3. Criminal investigation—History—Juvenile literature. I. Title. II. Series.
　　HV8073.8.Y68 2007
　　363.25—dc22　　2006001748

Chelsea House books are available at special discounts when purchased in bulk quantities for businesses, associations, institutions, or sales promotions. Please call our Special Sales Department in New York at (212) 967-8800 or (800) 322-8755.

You can find Chelsea House on the World Wide Web at http://www.chelseahouse.com

Text design by James Scotto-Lavino
Cover design by Dorothy M. Preston
Illustrations by Melissa Ericksen

Printed in the United States of America

VB Hermitage 10 9 8 7 6 5 4 3 2 1

This book is printed on acid-free paper.

CONTENTS

PREFACE

The Milestones in Science and Discovery set is based on a simple but powerful idea—that science and technology are not separate from people's daily lives. Rather, they are part of seeking to understand and reshape the world, an activity that virtually defines being human.

More than a million years ago, the ancestors of modern humans began to shape stones into tools that helped them compete with the specialized predators around them. Starting about 35,000 years ago, the modern type of human, *Homo sapiens,* also created elaborate cave paintings and finely crafted art objects, showing that technology had been joined with imagination and language to compose a new and vibrant world of culture. Humans were not only shaping their world but representing it in art and thinking about its nature and meaning.

Technology is a basic part of that culture. The mythologies of many peoples include a trickster figure, who upsets the settled order of things and brings forth new creative and destructive possibilities. In many myths, for instance, a trickster such as the Native Americans' Coyote or Raven steals fire from the gods and gives it to human beings. All technology, whether it harnesses fire, electricity, or the energy locked in the heart of atoms or genes, partakes of the double-edged gift of the trickster, providing power to both hurt and heal.

An inventor of technology is often inspired by the discoveries of scientists. Science as we know it today is younger than technology, dating back about 500 years to a period called the Renaissance. During the Renaissance, artists and thinkers began to explore nature systematically, and the first modern scientists, such as Leonardo da Vinci (1452–1519) and Galileo Galilei (1564–1642), used instruments and experiments to develop and test ideas about how objects in the universe behaved. A succession of revolutions followed, often introduced by individual geniuses: Isaac Newton (1643–1727) in mechanics and mathematics, Charles Darwin (1809–1882) in biological evolution, Albert Einstein (1879–1955) in relativity and quantum physics, James Watson (1928–   ) and Francis Crick (1916–2004) in modern genetics. Today's emerging fields of science and technology, such as genetic engineering, nanotechnology, and artificial intelligence, have their own inspiring leaders.

The fact that particular names such as Newton, Darwin, and Einstein can be so easily associated with these revolutions suggests the importance of the individual in modern science and technology. Each book in this set thus focuses on the lives and achievements of eight to 10 individuals who together have revolutionized an aspect of science or technology. Each book presents a different field: marine science, genetics, astronomy and space science, forensic science, communications technology, robotics, artificial intelligence, and mathematical simulation. Although early pioneers are included where appropriate, the emphasis is generally on researchers who worked in the 20th century or are still working today.

The biographies in each volume are placed in an order that reflects the flow of the individuals' major achievements, but these life stories are often intertwined. The achievements of particular men and women cannot be understood without some knowledge of the times they lived in, the people they worked with, and developments that preceded their research. Newton famously remarked, "If I have seen further [than others], it is by standing on the shoulders of giants." Each scientist or inventor builds upon—or wrestles with—the work that has come before. Individual scientists and inventors also interact with others in their own laboratories and elsewhere, sometimes even partaking in vast collective efforts, such as the government and private projects that raced at the end of the 20th century to complete the description of the human genome. Scientists and inventors affect, and are affected by, economic, political, and social forces as well. The relationship between scientific and technical creativity and developments in social institutions is another important facet of this series.

A number of additional features provide further context for the biographies in these books. Each chapter includes a chronology and suggestions for further reading. In addition, a glossary and a general bibliography (including organizations and Web resources) appear at the end of each book. Several types of sidebars are also used in the text to explore particular aspects of the profiled scientists' and inventors' work:

Connections Describes the relationship between the featured work and other scientific or technical developments.

I Was There Presents firsthand accounts of discoveries or inventions.

Issues Discusses scientific or ethical issues raised by the discovery or invention.

Other Scientists (or Inventors) Describes other individuals who played an important part in the work being discussed.

Parallels Shows parallel or related discoveries.

Social Impact Suggests how the discovery or invention affects or might affect society and daily life.

Solving Problems Explains how a scientist or inventor dealt with a particular technical problem or challenge.

Trends Presents data or statistics showing how developments in a field changed over time.

Our hope is that readers will be intrigued and inspired by these stories of the human quest for understanding, exploration, and innovation. We have tried to provide the context and tools to enable readers to forge their own connections and to further pursue their fields of interest.

ACKNOWLEDGMENTS

Thanks to the scientists in this book who reviewed their chapters and answered questions, and to the many scientists' assistants who patiently conveyed messages and sent (and sometimes re-sent) photographs, permission forms, and other items. My thanks, too, to my editor at Facts On File, Frank Darmstadt, for his help and good humor; to the copy editor, Amy L. Conver; to my cats, for providing purrs and not knocking the computer off my lap (though they tried); and, above all, to my husband, Harry Henderson, for unending support, love, and everything else that makes life good.

INTRODUCTION

Many people like to watch television programs in which scientists solve crimes, seemingly almost by magic. In these shows, latex-gloved technicians gather bits of hair, fiber, or blood from crime scenes and rush them to spotless laboratories. Lab workers in white coats place the samples under microscopes or feed them into mysterious machines. Other experts stare at computer screens and announce, "CODIS didn't turn up anything" or "I found a match on AFIS."

The lives of real forensic scientists—scientists who apply their skills to crimes or other legal matters—are not as glamorous as those of the television heroes, nor are their results as sure. They may need weeks or months to identify criminals or victims instead of hours, or they may never do so at all. However, they do share with TV characters such as *CSI*'s Gil Grissom a belief that the physical evidence found at a crime scene can reveal what happened there. Human witnesses may be absent, make mistakes, or hide information, but, as Grissom likes to say, "The evidence never lies."

Modern Forensic Science is one volume in Milestones in Discovery and Invention, a set of books by Facts On File. This set profiles key scientists in several fields, including both the pioneers who established each field and important scientists working in that specialty today. The set also describes these scientists' major discoveries and explains the importance of these discoveries to the science as a whole.

Chapter 1 features Mathieu Orfila, a Spanish-born French scientist who established the forensic science specialty of toxicology (the study of poisons) in 1813, and James T. Marsh, who invented a reliable test for the poison arsenic in 1836. These two men were among the first people to use the methods and equipment of science to solve crimes and identify criminals.

In the late 19th century, government officials in several European countries concluded that people who committed crimes repeatedly should be punished more severely than those who were first-time offenders. Identifying arrested people who had already been in prison thus became important. Renowned British scientist Francis Galton, a cousin of Charles Darwin, proposed in 1892 that the pattern of curving lines on a person's fingertips could be used for identification. He offered evidence to show that no two people had exactly the same "finger prints." A few years later, Edward Henry, a British official working in India, developed a practical classification system for fingerprints, and variations of Henry's system were adopted all over the Western world in the early 1900s. Galton and Henry are the chief subjects of chapter 2.

Other scientists realized that fingerprints were not the only identifiable signs that criminals or their victims could leave at a crime scene. Austrian physician Karl Landsteiner showed around 1900 that blood also differs from person to person. Landsteiner's discovery of blood types, outlined in chapter 3, was most important for providing a way to give blood transfusions safely, but it also benefited forensic science because other researchers found ways to determine blood type from small, dried blood drops or spatters. Landsteiner and other turn-of-the-century scientists founded serology, the study of blood and other bodily fluids (such as saliva, semen, and tears). Forensic serologists can use blood spots to determine not only the identity of people at a crime scene but also where they stood and how they moved.

Two Frenchmen, Alexandre Lacassagne and his pupil Edmond Locard, did perhaps more to establish forensic science as a whole than any others. They also took the first steps toward developing several of the fields in which forensic scientists specialize today, including forensic ballistics (the study of guns and bullets used in crimes) and forensic anthropology (the study of dead bodies, especially of bones). Chapter 4 tells the story of their advances.

Lacassagne and Locard showed that, as Locard put it in a famous saying, every contact leaves a trace. Without knowing it, every criminal leaves something behind at a crime scene—fingerprints, hair, fibers from clothing, or the casing from a spent bullet, for instance—and takes something away, such as dirt, leaves, or dust. Lacassagne and Locard solved a number of famous crimes by examining trace evidence, or small fragments of material, under a microscope. In 1910, Edmond Locard also set up the earliest laboratory dedicated to forensic science. Here, for the first time, physical evidence from crime scenes was studied systematically, using scientific principles.

Alexandre Lacassagne noticed that bullets and bullet casings have their own "fingerprints" in the form of marks made by gun barrels as the bullets pass through them. In the 1920s and 1930s, U.S. researcher Calvin Goddard developed ways to analyze and classify bullet markings, founding the specialty of forensic ballistics. As described in chapter 5, Goddard used bullet evidence to identify the people who committed several highly publicized crimes.

While Calvin Goddard was examining bullets, several inventors, most notably Berkeley (California) police officer Leonarde Keeler, were creating a machine that, they claimed, could help police determine whether a witness or suspect was telling the truth during an interrogation. This machine, the polygraph—popularly called the lie detector—measures blood pressure, breathing rate, and other bodily signs that change with stress, including the stress produced by attempts to deceive. As chapter 6 explains, judges and juries were suspicious of the polygraph when it was first introduced, and some experts still question its value. Police say, however, that the machine has often helped them obtain confessions and other information that would otherwise have remained hidden.

A second controversial forensic machine, perfected by Bell Telephone Laboratories engineer Lawrence Kersta in the early 1960s, is described in chapter 7. This machine, the sound spectrograph, analyzes recordings of spoken words. Kersta believed that individuals' voiceprints, as he termed them, are as unique as their fingerprints. Police have found voiceprints useful in identifying speakers who make telephoned bomb threats or ransom demands, but interpretation of sound spectrograms (the printouts made by the sound spectrograph) can be tricky. As with analysis of polygraph recordings, accuracy of voiceprint analysis seems to depend a great deal on the training and experience of the examiner.

Sometimes the only evidence that forensic scientists possess is a badly decayed corpse, a skull or skeleton, or a mere handful of bone fragments. Another group of specialists, forensic anthropologists, can make even these hard-to-read clues reveal the identity of a body and information about when and how the person died. Chapters 8 and 9 portray the careers of two forensic anthropologists, Clyde Snow and William Bass. Snow used his skill as a "bone detective" in the 1970s, 1980s, and 1990s to identify the victims of air crashes, serial killers, and governments who used mass murder as a political weapon. During the same period, William Bass and his students at the University of Tennessee's Anthropological Research Facility, informally called the Body Farm, developed tests that use the condition of a dead body to determine the person's time of death.

Beginning with the development of fingerprinting, forensic scientists realized that the human body provides the best tools for identifying criminals and crime victims. British researcher Alec Jeffreys, the subject of chapter 10, discovered in 1984 that the ultimate identifier is the genetic material that shapes life itself. Jeffreys showed that portions of the molecules of DNA (deoxyribonucleic acid), the substance of which genes are made, differ from person to person in ways as unique as the variations in fingerprints. Jeffreys's DNA profiling test has been called "the jewel in the crown of forensic science."

Whether they were pioneers or are experts working today, all the scientists described in *Modern Forensic Science* solved crimes by using observation and logical reasoning. They depended on observation to lead them to physical evidence at crime scenes and to help them decide which of the hundreds of fingerprints, hairs, fibers, stains, and other items they saw were out of place or likely to be important. They used reasoning to interpret what their senses and their machines told them and to draw conclusions about what happened during the crime and who the criminals or victims might be. They tested their conclusions by examining the evidence further or by asking what police found out from interviewing suspects and witnesses. If what they learned did not support their conclusions, they revised their ideas to fit what the evidence told them.

In other words, forensic scientists succeed—when they do— because they think the way all good scientists think. The skills of observation, reasoning, and testing ideas by experiment that forensic scientists apply to solving crimes and tracking criminals are the same ones that scientists of every type use to find out the truth about the world. In learning how forensic scientists work, readers can discover a great deal about science itself.

1

DEADLY POWDER

MATHIEU ORFILA, JAMES MARSH, AND DETECTION OF POISONS

Poison is everywhere. Many plants contain poisons, for example. Most household products and even medicines can be poisonous. As an early chemist who called himself Paracelsus stated in the 16th century, "All substances are poisons. . . . The right dose [makes the difference between] a poison and a remedy."

Until the 19th century, most poisons were undetectable as well as common, which meant that poisoners usually escaped punishment. Family members or neighbors might be suspect if an unloved wife or husband or a rich parent died suddenly, but no one could prove that such a person had been poisoned. As a result, historians say, poisoning was widespread in some places and times, such as in Italy and France in the late 1600s.

The most popular poison, contemporary accounts claim, was arsenic. The human body needs tiny amounts of this metallic element, but arsenic is poisonous in most doses. Arsenic was most commonly found in the form of arsenic oxide, a white powder that had respectable uses ranging from improving the complexion to poisoning rats. Because white arsenic, as the powder was called, was odorless and tasteless as well as easy to buy, however, some people applied it to less legitimate purposes. Secretly mixed into food, the powder caused stomach pains, vomiting, diarrhea, and other signs of illness just like the symptoms of cholera and several other common, deadly diseases. Only a minute dose of arsenic (about 0.009 ounce, or 0.25 g) was needed to kill a person. White arsenic was supposedly

1

Spanish-born Mathieu Orfila, working in France, founded the science of toxicology by writing an exhaustive book on poisons in 1813. (National Library of Medicine, photo B020198)

used so often to poison rich relatives in late 17th-century France that it was nicknamed "inheritance powder."

The reign of inheritance powder came to an end around 1840, thanks largely to two men: British chemist James Marsh, who developed a sensitive test for arsenic in human tissue, and Mathieu Orfila, a Spanish-born scientist working in France who almost single-handedly founded the science of toxicology. Toxicology is the study of poisons and their effects, including not only obvious poisons such as arsenic but also drugs (legal or illegal) and industrial chemicals. Identifying poisons and determining whether they were taken accidentally or purposefully for suicide or murder is a vital part of forensic science.

Founding a Science

Mathieu-Joseph-Bonaventure Orfila (known also as Mateu [Mathieu] Josep[h] Bonaventura Orfila i Rotger) was born on April 24, 1787, in Mahón, a town on Minorca, a small island off the coast of Spain. Orfila's early education came from local priests and the library of his merchant father. A child genius, Orfila could speak five languages by the time he was 14 years old.

Orfila initially planned to become a sailor, but he found his first sea journey (at age 15) boring and uncomfortable, and his interest turned toward medicine. Impressing his teachers at each stage of his training enough to obtain a scholarship to pay for the next stage, he studied in Valencia, Barcelona, Madrid, and, finally, Paris. He earned his medical degree in 1811.

Soon after his graduation, Orfila began giving private classes in chemistry to earn money. These classes became very popular, but Orfila sometimes had problems with his demonstrations. In April 1813, after he failed several times to show his students the precipitate (solid matter) that was supposed to form when arsenic acid was mixed with various substances—a common test for arsenic at the time—he decided to examine other standard tests for poisons in fluids such as soup, wine, and coffee. He found that most of the tests were unreliable. Scientists could detect many poisons, he learned, only by feeding suspect substances to animals and waiting to see whether the animals died. "The central fact that had struck me had never been perceived by anyone else," he wrote later. "My first words were these: *Toxicology does not yet exist.*"

Orfila set out to change that fact by writing the first scientific book on the subject, *Traité des poisons* (Treatise on poisons). The book divided poisons into several groups and described their effects on the living body, the symptoms of illness they produce, the signs they leave in a dead body, and the ways of identifying them. The first volume of this exhaustive work appeared later in 1813, the second volume in 1815. "Its impact was immediate and tremendous," Colin and Damon Wilson write in *Written in Blood: A History of Forensic Detection*. Essentially, they say, Orfila founded the science of toxicology with this book. Orfila later wrote several other books and numerous papers on poisons, medical chemistry, and medical jurisprudence, as forensic science was then called.

Traité des poisons made Orfila famous, and he rose rapidly in the academic world. He became professor of "mental maladies" in the medical school of Paris, a post created just for him, in 1818. A year later, he took over the medical school's professorship of medical jurisprudence. He succeeded famous chemist Louis-Nicolas Vauquelin, who had trained him, as professor of chemistry in 1823 and became dean of the medical school in 1830.

During these years, Orfila became one of the first scientists to appear as an expert witness in trials. He testified in a court for the first time in August 1824. The defendant in that trial was a woman named Laurent, who had been charged with killing her husband after a local physician said he found arsenic in the dead man's body.

When Orfila retested the husband's stomach, however, he found no poison, and the widow Laurent was acquitted.

A Sensitive Test

Mathieu Orfila was a brilliant chemist, but he was not the person who created a sensitive, dependable test for arsenic, the substance that had given him such trouble in his 1813 chemistry demonstration. That achievement came from a more obscure man, British chemist James Marsh.

Marsh was born on September 2, 1794, but little is known of his early life beyond this fact. He became a chemist at London's Woolwich Arsenal and the associated Royal Military Academy in 1822, working to improve military guns and cannons. From 1829 to 1846, he also assisted Michael Faraday, another employee of the Royal Military Academy, who became famous for research on electricity and the discovery of the relationship between electricity and magnetism.

Marsh did not have Orfila's reputation as an expert witness, but in December 1832, Marsh was also called to testify at a poisoning trial. A man named John Bodle had been arrested for murdering his grandfather, George, by putting arsenic in the old man's coffee, and the judge at Bodle's trial asked Marsh to test George Bodle's stomach for the poison because Marsh was the most qualified chemist in the area. Marsh used a test that was supposed to produce a yellow precipitate if arsenic was present. The precipitate appeared, but by the time he showed it to the jury, the powder had broken down and no longer showed an obvious color. The jury found the test unconvincing and acquitted Bodle.

Marsh, who believed that Bodle was guilty (a suspicion proved correct 10 years later, when Bodle, then safely out of the country, confessed to the crime), was frustrated that he had not had clearer evidence to show the jury. He decided to invent a more dependable and sensitive test for arsenic in the human body.

The best known of the tests for arsenic used at the time was the "arsenic mirror," which Johann Metzger, a medical professor in Königsberg (Kaliningrad), Germany, had invented in 1787. Metzger showed that if a mixture containing arsenic was heated until it turned red, a layer of black metallic arsenic would be deposited on any nearby cold surface, such as a plate. Metzger called this layer the arsenic mirror because it was shiny. Metzger's reaction by itself could not detect arsenic in a body, but, in 1806, Valentine Rose, a professor at the Berlin School of Medicine, developed a way to treat a human stomach and its contents so that the mirror test could be applied to them.

MARSH TEST APPARATUS

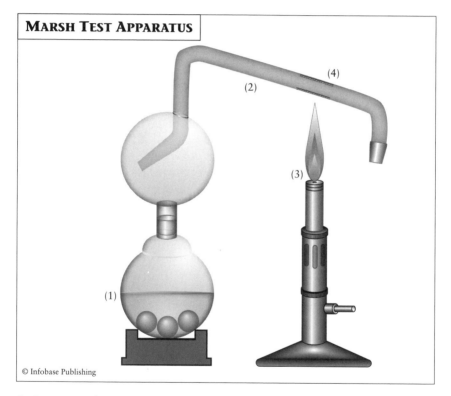

© Infobase Publishing

In James Marsh's sensitive test for arsenic, the material to be tested was mixed with zinc and sulfuric acid in the small flask at the left (1). If the sample contained arsenic, hydrogen from the acid combined with the arsenic to form arsine gas. The gas passed into the horizontal tube (2). Near the end of the tube, the gas was heated by a flame (3). The heat broke down the arsine and released metallic arsenic, which formed a black, shiny deposit (called the arsenic mirror) at the end of the tube (4).

Metzger's and Rose's tests often failed to detect small amounts of arsenic. In the most common form of the tests, arsenic in the material being tested was converted into a poisonous, garlicky-smelling gas called arsine, a combination of arsenic and hydrogen, before being heated. James Marsh realized that much of the arsine probably escaped into the air before it could drop its load of arsenic. If only a small amount of arsenic was present in the test material, too little might be left to form the arsenic mirror.

To end this difficulty, Marsh created a closed apparatus that kept the gas confined. He combined the material being tested with zinc and sulfuric acid in a flask that opened into a narrow, horizontal tube. If the material contained arsenic, the arsenic would react with hydrogen in the acid and produce arsine gas, which passed into the tube. A flame beneath the tube heated the gas, making it break down into hydrogen and metallic arsenic. When the arsenic reached a cold part of the tube, it formed the characteristic black "mirror."

Marsh's test was so sensitive that it could detect 0.0000007 ounce (.02 mg) of arsenic in a sample. He described his invention in "The Test for Arsenic," published in the *Edinburgh Philosophical Journal* in October 1836. The Society of Arts awarded him a gold medal for his work. Marsh later improved the test to allow the amount of arsenic in the sample to be measured by comparing the length of the metallic arsenic deposit in the thin tube with the lengths of deposits made by known amounts of arsenic. The tube containing the test deposit could be sealed and later displayed to a jury as evidence.

Pretty Poisoner

Mathieu Orfila's expertise in toxicology and James Marsh's new test for arsenic came together in September 1840 during the trial of Marie Lafarge, a figure in one of the most highly publicized courtroom dramas of the day. Marie had been married to Charles Lafarge, a master ironworker. She had had no say in her choice of husband, and the marriage was not a happy one. Charles Lafarge died on January 16, 1840, after suffering severe stomach problems that began when he ate a piece of cake that his wife made for him. Nine days after Charles's death, 24-year-old Marie was arrested and charged with his murder.

Suspicion about Charles's illness began even before he died. A maidservant who worked for the Lafarge family told Lafarge's mother and doctor that she had seen Marie putting white powder into milk, soup, and eggnog that the young woman then fed to her husband. When Charles Lafarge died, the family and the physician told authorities about their suspicions.

The examining magistrate (a judge who performed some functions of a detective) learned that Marie had bought white arsenic, supposedly for poisoning rats, a few days before Charles first became ill. He ordered Charles's body to be brought out of its grave and tested for arsenic, and he told the police to arrest Marie. Her arrest made headlines in the Paris newspapers because Marie, in addition to being attractive, was related to members of France's nobility, including the royal family.

Marie Lafarge's trial began in the city of Tulle on September 3, 1840. Marie and her wealthy relatives insisted that she was innocent, but the evidence against her appeared strong. Several local chemists testified that they had found arsenic in the box from which the maid had seen Marie take the white powder. Arsenic was also in the milk, the eggnog, and Charles Lafarge's vomit and stomach contents.

Marie Lafarge's defense lawyer contacted Orfila, who by then was considered Europe's foremost expert on poisons. Orfila, unlike most other chemists of the time, knew about the Marsh test for arsenic and had been using it for several years. After reading the Tulle chemists' report, Orfila complained that they had used older, less reliable tests and had performed the tests so badly that the results were worthless.

When the defense attorney read Orfila's comments in court, the prosecution's lawyers offered to have the chemists apply the Marsh test to the suspect materials as well. After doing so, the chemists reported that the foods and the powder in the box still showed high amounts of arsenic. The scientists admitted, however, that they could not find clear evidence of arsenic in Charles Lafarge's stomach or other organs.

The trial judge finally asked Orfila himself to come to Tulle and settle the issue. Orfila arrived on September 13 and, with the local chemists watching, repeated the Marsh test on all the materials that night. The next afternoon, he told the packed courthouse, "I shall

In 1840, Mathieu Orfila was an expert witness in the highly publicized murder trial of Marie Lafarge, shown here. Orfila used the Marsh test to show that the body of Lafarge's husband contained arsenic, and this evidence led to her conviction. (Roger-Viollet, photo 7951-14)

prove that there is arsenic in the body of [Charles] Lefarge, and that this arsenic cannot have found its way there from the soil" in which Lafarge's body had lain. (Two years before, Orfila had shown that arsenic exists naturally in the soil of some cemeteries and can seep into bodies that are carelessly buried.) Orfila went on to state that he had found arsenic not only in Lafarge's stomach but also in numerous other parts of his body. Marie Lafarge was found guilty of murder on September 19 and sentenced to life in prison.

The Lafarge affair was the first major court case in which scientific tests and the testimony of expert witnesses played a key part. The trial made the Marsh test famous, and chemists began demonstrating it in lectures and even at parties. The popularity of the Marsh test combined with changes in European laws to make poisoning by arsenic much less common. In 1851, for example, Britain passed the Arsenic Act, which allowed druggists to sell poisons, particularly arsenic, only to people whom they knew personally. Individuals who bought poison also had to sign a "poison book" as a record of their purchases. Arsenic oxide sold as rat poison had to be colored with soot (coal dust) or indigo, a dark blue dye, to keep the powder from being confused, accidentally or otherwise, with sugar or flour.

A Legacy of Students

Some people questioned Mathieu Orfila's conclusions in the Marie Lafarge case, but no criticism could damage his high reputation.

CONNECTIONS: WAS NAPOLÉON POISONED?

Napoléon Bonaparte (1769–1821) ruled France as First Consul of the French Republic (1799–1804) and then as Emperor Napoléon I (1804–14). After conquering large parts of Europe in a series of wars, he was defeated at the Battle of the Nations, near Leipzig, Germany, in 1813. He was forced to give up his throne and was exiled to the island of Elba, but supporters helped him escape, and he briefly regained control of France. The British defeated him decisively at the Battle of Waterloo on June 18, 1815. This time, he was sent to St. Helena, a volcanic island in the remote South Atlantic. He died there on May 5, 1821.

Napoléon's body was given an autopsy, a medical examination intended to determine the cause of his death. The physicians who performed the autopsy concluded that the former emperor had died of stomach cancer. In 1952, however, Sten Forshufvud, a Swedish dentist with a strong interest in Napoléon's history, proposed that some of the deposed ruler's attendants, probably paid by people who wanted to make sure that the exile did not make another try for power, had slowly poisoned him with arsenic. Forshufvud said that the symptoms of Napoléon's last illness could be explained just as easily by arsenic poisoning as by cancer.

Arsenic is known to accumulate in hair, and samples of Napoléon's hair had been preserved. Forshufvud obtained one of these in the 1960s and sent it to Hamilton Smith, a forensic toxicologist at Glasgow University in Scotland. Using the neutron activation test, an extremely sensitive test for arsenic that Smith himself had developed, the toxicologist found levels of arsenic in the hair that were well above normal.

The fact that Napoléon's body contained arsenic does not prove that he was poisoned deliberately, however. David Jones, a chemist at the University of Newcastle, England, pointed out in 1980 that the arsenic could have come from wallpaper in the house where Napoléon lived. A green dye often used in wallpaper at the time contained an arsenic compound that could be dissolved by mold, converting some of the arsenic to poisonous arsine gas. The gas would not have been strong enough to kill the ex-emperor, but he could have breathed in enough arsenic to make his other stomach problems worse and hasten his death. Historians still disagree about whether arsenic played a role in Napoléon's death and, if it did, whether the poison was given to him on purpose or absorbed accidentally.

Orfila received numerous honors and promotions during the decade that followed the trial, even serving as King Louis XVIII's personal physician for a while. His rewards came to an end, however, when France became a republic in 1848. Orfila died in Paris on March 12, 1853, after a short illness.

Orfila left behind not only his own considerable research but also a group of former students who had become almost as famous in forensic toxicology as he was. For instance, Alfred Swaine Taylor, who had studied under Orfila in Paris, was professor of medical jurisprudence at Guy's Hospital medical school in London. Taylor published *Principles and Practice of Medical Jurisprudence,* the field's first textbook in English, in 1836, the same year that James Marsh developed his arsenic test.

Jean-Servais Stas, another former student of Orfila's, became a professor of chemistry at the royal military school in Brussels, Belgium, and solved a problem that Orfila himself had thought hopeless: the detection of plant-based poisons, including narcotics such as opium (from the opium poppy) and alkaloids such as belladonna, or atropine (from the deadly nightshade plant). These natural substances break down in the body very quickly, seemingly leaving no trace.

In a famous Belgian trial in 1850, Stas demonstrated the presence of nicotine, a powerful alkaloid poison from tobacco plants, in the body of Gustave Fougnies, a wealthy man who had died suddenly. After repeated purification of Fougnies's stomach contents, Stas mixed the remaining extract with liquid ether, into which the poison dissolved. Ether weighs less than water, so the ether formed a layer above the water in the test liquid, carrying the poison with it. Stas poured the ether into a separate dish and let it evaporate. What remained was an oily, colorless liquid that smelled strongly of tobacco. Stas used accepted chemical tests to demonstrate that the liquid was nicotine. The trial revealed that Fougnies's sister and her husband, Count Hyppolyte de Bocarmé, had extracted the poison from tobacco plants and poured it down Fougnies's throat. Toxicologists adapted Stas's procedure to reveal other deadly alkaloids.

Unlike Mathieu Orfila, James Marsh received little recognition for his work. Marsh died on June 21, 1846, leaving a widow, two children, and no money. The British government gave the widow a small yearly income in honor of her husband's contributions to science.

Modern Poison Detection

In the early 20th century, the Marsh test was refined to the point that it could detect as little as 0.0000000007 ounce (1 µg, or 1 millionth of a gram) of arsenic in body tissue. This and other 19th-century tests for poison were eventually replaced by more advanced technologies. Many of these new methods have the advantage of not destroying the sample, as older chemical tests such as the Marsh test did. They can also detect tiny amounts of poison and work with very small samples. Today's forensic toxicologists can look for poison not only in stomach contents but also in blood, urine, hair, or almost any other material from the body.

One of the most popular tests for poisoning uses a combination of two technologies, gas chromatography and mass spectrometry. Chromatography separates the substances in a mixture. In gas chromatography, the mixture is vaporized, or turned into gas, and then sent through a coiled glass tube. The mass spectrometer bombards the gas with electrons, breaking them into electrically charged fragments with different masses (weight). A computer program determines the masses automatically and produces a readout that shows what chemicals the mixture contained and in what proportions.

No doubt at least partly because of toxicologists' success in identifying poisons, poisoning has become a relatively rare way to commit murder. The FBI has stated that out of 14,121 homicides in 2004, only 11 were the result of poisoning. However, Robert Middleberg of National Medical Services, an independent toxicology laboratory, told Court TV writer Katherine Ramsland that he suspects that the number of poisonings is underestimated. Poisoners today must use toxins more subtle than "inheritance powder," but their race against forensic toxicologists is sure to continue.

Chronology

| 1787 | Mathieu-Joseph-Bonaventure Orfila born in Mahón, Minorca, Spain, on April 24 |
| | Johann Metzger invents "arsenic mirror" test for arsenic |

1794	James Marsh born in Britain on September 2
1806	Valentine Rose invents method for applying arsenic mirror test to human stomach contents
1811	Orfila earns medical degree in Paris
1813	After a failed demonstration of a test for arsenic, Orfila begins studying poisons and methods for identifying them; later in the year, he publishes first volume of his *Traité des poisons* (Treatise on Poisons)
1815	Second volume of *Traité des poisons* published
1818	Orfila becomes professor of mental maladies at Paris medical school
1819	Orfila becomes professor of medical jurisprudence
1822	Marsh becomes chemist at Woolwich Arsenal and Royal Military Academy in London
1823	Orfila becomes professor of chemistry at the medical school
1824	In August, Orfila testifies as an expert witness in a trial for the first time
1829–46	Marsh assists Michael Faraday
1830	Orfila becomes dean of the medical school
1832	Marsh testifies in the John Bodle trial in December; the jury rejects his evidence
1836	In October, Marsh publishes a description of his new test for arsenic in *Edinburgh Philosophical Journal*
	Alfred Swaine Taylor, a former student of Orfila's, publishes *Principles and Practice of Medical Jurisprudence,* the first forensic medicine textbook in English
1840	In September, Orfila uses Marsh test to prove the guilt of Marie Lafarge in a highly publicized poisoning trial
1840s	Orfila receives honors and promotions and serves as King Louis XVIII's personal physician

1846	Marsh dies on June 21
1848	France becomes a republic; Orfila's loses influence
1850	Jean-Servais Stas, another former student of Orfila's, detects an alkaloid (nicotine) in stomach contents for the first time
1851	Britain passes Arsenic Act
1853	Orfila dies in Paris on March 12 after a short illness

Further Reading

Books

Orfila, Mathieu. *Traité des poisons.* 2 vols. Paris: Chez Crochard, 1813, 1815.
> Orfila's work on poisons, their effects on the body, the symptoms they cause, and the means of identifying them; this book essentially established the field of toxicology.

Taylor, Alfred Swaine. *Principles and Practice of Medical Jurisprudence.* London: publisher unknown, 1836.
> First forensic medicine textbook in English, written by a former student of Orfila.

Wilson, Colin, and Damon Wilson. *Written in Blood: A History of Forensic Detection.* New York: Carroll & Graf, reissue, 2003.
> Contains an extensive chapter on poisoning and toxicology that includes material on Mathieu Orfila and James Marsh.

Yeatts, Tabatha. *Forensics: Solving the Crime.* Minneapolis: Oliver Press, 2001.
> For young adults. Contains a chapter on James Marsh.

Articles

Cotton, Simon. "Arsine." Available online. URL: http://www.chm.bris.ac.uk/motm/arsine/arsineh.htm. Accessed on September 24, 2005.
> Lively question-and-answer discussion of arsenic poisoning and the chemistry of arsine gas, including references to Mathieu Orfila and the Marsh test for arsenic.

Marsh, James. "The Test for Arsenic." *Edinburgh Philosophical Journal,* October 1836.
Scientific article in which James Marsh described his new test for arsenic.

Ramsland, Katherine. "Forensic Toxicology." Available online. URL: http://www.crimelibrary.com/criminal_mind/forensics/toxicology. Accessed on September 22, 2005.
Series of 14 articles on forensic toxicology, part of Court TV's Crime Library, that discusses both historical cases (including the Lafarge case and the debate about whether Napoléon Bonaparte was poisoned) and modern ones, as well as early and modern methods of poison detection.

2

ARCHES, LOOPS, AND WHORLS

FRANCIS GALTON, EDWARD HENRY, AND FINGERPRINTING

The work of police, judges, and juries would be much easier if criminals left signed confessions at the scenes of their crimes. That seldom happens, of course, but criminals often do leave identifying "signatures" in the form of fingerprints. No two people, not even identical twins, have ever been shown to have exactly the same pattern of raised, curved lines on their fingertips. Oily sweat produced by tiny glands coats the fingertips and leaves imprints of this unique pattern on almost any surface. Forensic scientists can reveal these impressions at the scene of a crime and, with the help of computers, match the prints to those of suspects or known criminals.

In the late 19th century, a series of British administrative officials and scientists showed how fingerprints could be used to identify people and solve crimes. The two who did the most to make fingerprinting practical were Francis Galton and Edward Henry.

Wordless Signatures

People have remarked on fingerprints and their possible uniqueness since ancient times. The Chinese used fingerprints as signatures on contracts about 2,000 years ago. In 1788, a German scientist, J.

15

British scientist Francis Galton, a cousin of Charles Darwin, developed the first extensive classification system for fingerprints and provided evidence that each person's fingerprints are unique. (National Library of Medicine, photo B012611)

C. Mayer, claimed in an anatomy textbook, "the arrangement of skin ridges [on the fingers] is never duplicated in two persons." Czech anatomy professor Jan Evangelista Purkyně divided fingerprints into nine types in a book about the skin published in 1823. These and other early researchers saw the differences in fingerprints mostly as a scientific curiosity.

Like the ancient Chinese, the first person to use fingerprints in connection with crime, William James Herschel, pictured them as a kind of signature. Herschel, descendant of a renowned family of British scientists (his grandfather, also named William, had discovered the planet Uranus in 1781), was a civil servant in India, which Britain controlled during the 19th century.

Herschel found that people in Bengal, the Indian province in which he worked, sometimes signed contracts and later denied that the signatures were theirs. In July 1858, hoping to prevent this problem, Herschel asked Rajyadhar Konai, a Bengali road contractor, to sign a contract with a print of his palm, coated in ink, as well as a written signature. He showed Konai the differences between the lines on Konai's palm and those on his own and told the Bengali that Konai would never be able to deny his signature because his handprint would identify him. Konai apparently was impressed enough to honor his agreement.

When Herschel became a magistrate (judge) in Nuddea, near Calcutta, in 1860, he encouraged the use of fingerprint signatures on other types of documents often involved in fraud, such as land rental agreements and receipts for government pension payments. He also began collecting and studying the fingerprints of family members, friends and acquaintances, and people he met in his administrative work. He found that each person's prints were different from all the others and that an individual's prints did not change with age.

In 1877, Herschel, then magistrate of Hooghly, also near Calcutta, ordered that the prints of two fingers be used instead of written signatures on all pensions, deeds, and jail warrants. He thus became the first modern person to put fingerprints to regular, official use. Herschel retired and moved back to England in 1878, and the man who replaced him discontinued his fingerprint system.

Mark of a Thief

About the time William Herschel was leaving India, another Briton began to share Herschel's fascination with the ridges and furrows of the hand. This man was Henry Faulds, a Scottish Presbyterian missionary and physician who had established a hospital in Tsukiji, Japan, in 1875. Around 1878, while visiting an archaeological site near the hospital, Faulds noticed small patterns of parallel lines in fragments of ancient pottery and realized to his amazement that he was seeing marks left by the fingers of the potters.

Just as Herschel had done in India about 20 years earlier, Faulds (who had never heard of Herschel's activities) began collecting and examining the fingerprints of everyone he met. Unlike Herschel, who had taken only one or two prints from each person, Faulds made inked impressions of all 10 fingers. He and some of his medical students also scraped the ridges from their fingers with knives, acid, sandpaper, or other abrasives as an experiment. Each time, they found, the prints grew back in exactly the same pattern as before. Fingerprints appeared to be permanent features of each person's body.

Around 1880, Faulds used the uniqueness of fingerprints to identify criminals who had committed several local thefts, something Herschel had never thought of doing. Faulds matched handprints or fingerprints left at the sites of the burglaries to those in his collection. He also convinced police of the innocence of a man whom they had suspected of one of the crimes by showing that the man's handprint did not look like the print left on a whitewashed fence next to the burgled house.

Faulds described his experiences in a letter to *Nature,* a prestigious European science journal. His letter, titled "On the Skin-furrows of the Hand," was published on October 28, 1880. In it, Faulds described two types of fingerprint patterns, loops (formed when the ridges running from one side of the fingertip to the other turn back on themselves) and whorls (formed when the ridges turn through at least one complete circle).

"Enough had been observed," Faulds wrote, "to enable me confidently, as a practical biologist, to assert the invariableness, for practical identification purposes, of the patterns formed by the lineations of human fingertips." He suggested that detectives might use "bloody finger-marks or impressions on clay, glass, etc." at crime scenes for "the scientific identification of criminals," just as he had done in Japan. He recommended that police keep a register of the "forever unchangeable finger-furrows of important criminals" so that such people could be identified if they repeated their crimes.

William Herschel read Faulds's letter and immediately wrote a reply, describing his own use of fingerprints as substitutes for signatures in India. *Nature* printed Herschel's letter on November 25, 1880. This exchange marked the start of a feud that the two men continued for much of the rest of their lives. Each insisted that he was the true inventor of fingerprinting.

A Society of Strangers

Faulds's and Herschel's letters attracted little attention when they appeared in *Nature.* Changes in society, however, soon made the men's discoveries important.

By the late 19th century, life in Europe and North America had become very different from life a century or two earlier. Throughout most of history, travel was difficult, and most people spent all their lives in the same town or village. The need to identify someone almost never arose because neighbors knew one another so well. In the early 19th century, however, the Industrial Revolution made travel easier and also gave people reasons to leave their birth homes. Huge numbers migrated to large cities to look for jobs that no longer existed in the countryside.

This movement, combined with a rise in total population, packed cities with people who were strangers to one another. Individuals could claim any name or background they wished, with little chance that anyone would deny their statements. Some criminals took advantage of this anonymity to commit fraud, for instance, by pretending to be wealthy businessmen in order to swindle investors out of their money.

Other criminals took false names, or aliases, to hide their past activities. In the second half of the 19th century, European scientists and law experts came to believe that people who committed crimes repeatedly should be given longer sentences for the same crime than those who performed a criminal act for the first time. This different treatment gave repeat offenders a motive to hide their identities from police and judges by taking new names and claiming to be first-timers.

Experienced police officers and local magistrates sometimes recognized criminals they had seen before, but they had little chance of identifying a repeater who came from a different part of the country. Police departments in some cities kept files of criminals' physical descriptions (noting, for instance, height, eye color, and unusual marks such as scars or tattoos), but the descriptions were often so vague that the files were of little use. Such files, furthermore, were usually indexed according to the criminal's name, so when criminals adopted aliases, their files probably would not be found. Dependence on personal recognition or on unclear descriptions also meant that innocent people who happened to look like known criminals were sometimes arrested and even sent to prison.

Measuring Criminals

In the 1880s, Alphonse Bertillon, a young clerk in the Paris police department, convinced a growing number of law enforcement leaders that he had developed an answer to the problem of identifying career criminals: measurement of different parts of the body, a procedure called anthropometry. Bertillon chose 11 measurements, such as head size and arm length, that seemed unlikely to alter with age or changes in weight. After testing prisoners in the late 1870s, he concluded that the odds of two people matching each other in any particular measurement were about one in four. The odds of their having all 11 measurements the same, therefore, were one in 4,194,304. For all practical purposes, Bertillon said, his system could distinguish between any two people.

Most important, the young Frenchman developed a filing system based on a classification of physical features rather than on names. He defined categories of large, medium, and small for seven of his measurements, starting with head size, as well as seven gradations of eye color. Within each category of head size, files were subdivided according to a similar classification of another measurement, and so on. Using this system, an officer could pick a handful of likely matches for a newly arrested criminal from a collection of thousands of files in just a few minutes.

In 1884, the first full year during which the Paris police used anthropometry, Bertillon's group identified 241 repeat criminals, far more than were usually found through personal recognition. The French national prison system officially adopted what came to be known as the Bertillon system in 1885, and police forces in the United States and Canada began using it in 1887.

Anthropometry worked much better than the techniques for identifying criminals that police had previously used, but it also had serious drawbacks. Taking the measurements on which the Bertillon system depended was time-consuming and difficult. The measurements were reliable only if the prisoners cooperated and the measurers followed Bertillon's written instructions exactly. Measurers, however, often misunderstood the instructions, skipped steps that they found tiresome, or added their own variations to the system. When measurements were inaccurate, identifications based on them naturally became undependable as well.

Scientific Study

One of the people who heard about Bertillon's achievements was Francis Galton, a respected British scientist. Like William Herschel,

OTHER SCIENTISTS: ALPHONSE BERTILLON (1853–1914)

Born in Paris on April 24, 1853, Alphonse Bertillon came from a family of anthropologists, or scientists who study differences between human beings. Indeed, Alphonse's father, Louis-Adolphe Bertillon, and his maternal grandfather, Achille Guillard, were among the founders of this scientific field and the related field of demography, the study of races and regional groups. They and other anthropologists used anthropometry, invented by Belgian statistician Lambert-Adolphe-Jacques Quételet, to explore differences among human populations, and Alphonse learned the technique from them in his youth.

In spite of his intelligence, Bertillon's hot temper and other personal problems made staying in school or keeping a job difficult. Only after his famous father supported his ideas about body measurement as a way of identifying criminals did he gain the opportunity to test his system in 1882.

Bertillon was famous during the late 1880s and early 1890s. His most spectacular success came in 1892, when anthropometry helped the Paris police discover that a bomber who called himself Ravachol was really François Koenigstein, a career criminal who had committed several murders. Koenigstein was executed, and Bertillon was awarded the Legion of Honor.

When fingerprinting began to replace anthropometry in the early 1900s, Bertillon had trouble adjusting to the change. He welcomed the addition of fingerprints to the "Bertillon cards" containing criminals' measurements and descriptions, but he felt that his classification system should remain supreme. He died a bitter man in Switzerland in 1914.

Bertillon might have felt less disappointed if he could have known that forms of anthropometry are still used. Some security systems work by measuring and recognizing unique features of the body, such as the shading and patterns in the iris (colored part) of the eye. Using calipers and other tools that Bertillon would have recognized, forensic anthropologists measure bones in a skeleton to determine the sex, race, age, and height of the person from whom the bones came.

Galton, born in 1822 in Sparkbrook, England, came from a famous and wealthy family that included several other scientists. Galton's best-known relative was his cousin, Charles Darwin, whose theory of evolution by natural selection, described in *On the Origin of Species* (published in 1859), triggered a storm of controversy because it contradicted many people's religious beliefs.

Galton explored many types of scientific work. As a young man, for instance, he explored part of southwestern Africa (now Namibia) and wrote two travel books. He invented weather mapping and made other contributions to meteorology, the study of weather. A founder of the science of statistics, Galton tried to describe every aspect of humanity mathematically, including women's beauty and the power of prayer. He was a member of the Royal Society, Britain's most admired scientific organization, and the almost equally prestigious Royal Geographic Society, from which he won a gold medal in 1853.

Like Charles Darwin, Galton was interested in the inheritance of characteristics, or traits. Galton focused on the traits of humans, including not only physical abilities but also mental traits such as intelligence and the tendency to commit crimes. Galton felt sure that such characteristics were inherited. He first wrote about his theory in *Hereditary Genius,* a book published in 1869. In this book, he claimed that famous and highly regarded people were usually descended from parents with those same characteristics.

Galton wanted to find physical markers that were inherited along with certain mental characteristics and could be used to identify people with those traits. He began studying anthropometry in 1884, measuring the physical characteristics and powers (such as grip strength and keenness of eyesight) of thousands of volunteers. In the late 1880s, Galton began to think that fingerprints might be the markers he was looking for.

Galton's research on fingerprints led him to the letters in *Nature* that Henry Faulds and William Herschel had written in 1880. Galton was interested to see that Faulds had mentioned the possibility of fingerprint patterns being inherited. For reasons that are not entirely clear, however, Galton wrote to Herschel (on March 1, 1888) rather than Faulds for more information. Herschel agreed to let Galton use his fingerprint collection, which by that time was immense, if Galton would give Herschel credit for having invented fingerprinting.

During the next four years, Galton studied fingerprints in a more systematic and scientific way than Faulds or Herschel had done. He assembled his own fingerprint collection, which eventually included about 8,000 sets of prints. He confirmed Herschel's conclusion that fingerprint patterns do not change with age and calculated that the chance of two whole fingerprints being identical was one in 64 billion.

Galton also worked out a system for classifying fingerprints. He divided loops into outer or inner, depending on whether the bottom of the loop opened outward (toward the thumb) or inward (toward the other fingers). In addition to whorls and two types of loops, his system included arches, in which the ridges do not turn, as they do in loops and whorls. Galton also noticed that fingerprint ridges

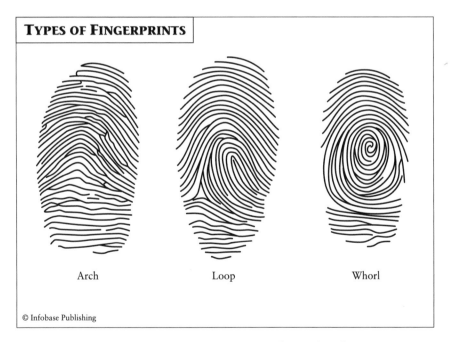

TYPES OF FINGERPRINTS

Arch	Loop	Whorl

© Infobase Publishing

The three main types of fingerprints in Francis Galton's classification system are arches, loops, and whorls.

FINGERPRINT MINUTIAE

Ridge ending

Enclosure

Bifurcation

Island

© Infobase Publishing

Galton subdivided fingerprints on the basis of small variations that he called ridge minutiae. Four types of minutiae are shown here.

contain many tiny variations, such as breaks or connections with other ridges. Comparison of these ridge minutiae, as he called them, let him distinguish between fingerprints with similar overall patterns, such as those of identical twins.

Galton described his research and classification system in a book called *Finger Prints,* which was published in 1892. He claimed that fingerprints classified by his system could be used to identify not only criminals but also military recruits, missing persons, and even travelers. He admitted, however, that he had

Social Impact: Eugenics

Breeders of cattle, horses, and other domestic animals deliberately mate individuals with characteristics that the breeders and their customers admire, such as strength or speed. Francis Galton felt that human beings should be their own breeders, choosing marriage partners on the basis of characteristics that would improve human stock if they were passed on to children. "As it is easy . . . to obtain . . . a permanent breed of dogs or horses gifted with peculiar powers of running . . . , so it would be quite practicable to produce a highly-gifted race of men," he wrote in *Hereditary Genius.* On the other hand, Galton maintained, people possessing traits that he and his social class thought undesirable—which were often features of races and ethnic groups other than upper-class Caucasians—should be discouraged from having children.

Galton named this doctrine *eugenics,* after Greek words meaning "well born." During the first decade of the 20th century, he founded a society to promote eugenics and spent most of his time popularizing this belief. Eugenics societies in Britain, the United States, and Germany attracted many members, including respected scientists and such well-known figures as Theodore Roosevelt, George Bernard Shaw, and (in his youth) Winston Churchill.

Eugenics supporters in the 1920s and 1930s emphasized negative eugenics—not merely discouraging, but forcibly preventing, "undesirable" people from having children. Groups held to be undesirable included the developmentally disabled, the insane, and habitual criminals. By the 1930s, some 34 states in the United States had passed laws requiring members of these groups to be forcibly sterilized (surgically made unable to reproduce). Denmark, Finland, Norway, Sweden, and some Canadian provinces enacted similar laws.

Nazi Germany carried negative eugenics to its greatest extreme. The German legislature passed a eugenic sterilization law soon after Adolf Hitler's party took power in 1933. During World War II, in an effort to create a "master race" of pure German descent, the Nazis tried to wipe out the genes of Jews, Gypsies, and other non-Germanic groups through mass killing. Germany's excesses produced a reaction against eugenics after the war, but eugenics laws in several countries and states remained in effect (though not necessarily enforced) until the 1970s.

As scientists learn more about humankind's genetic makeup and become more able to change genes at will, some people fear—or hope—that eugenics will be reborn in a new form. In the future, they say, parents may gain the power to choose the traits that their children will inherit. The effects of such choices could profoundly change society and even alter the definition of humanity.

Around 1897, Edward Henry and his associates in India developed the fingerprint classification system that most countries adopted in the early 20th century. (Metropolitan police, London)

failed to achieve his original aim of linking fingerprint patterns to particular races or to physical and mental characteristics.

A Better System

In 1892, soon after Galton's book on fingerprints was published, William Herschel sent it to Henry Cotton, an old friend in India. Cotton, then chief secretary to the government of Bengal, in turn passed the book to the heads of several government departments. One official who received a copy was Edward Richard Henry, Bengal's inspector-general of police.

Henry had been born in Shadwell, Wapping, London, on July 26, 1850. He graduated from University College, London, in 1869 and entered the Indian civil service in 1873. He became inspector-general in April 1891. He ordered police offices throughout the province to begin using a form of Alphonse Bertillon's anthropometry in 1892, but he found that training officers to make accurate measurements was difficult.

After reading Galton's book, Henry ordered thumbprints to be added to criminals' files. He began requiring prints of all 10 fingers in 1894. Henry met Galton in that same year during a trip to England, and the two agreed to work together. Galton promised to keep Henry informed about improvements that Galton was planning to make in his fingerprint classification system. Henry, in turn, said he would send convicts' fingerprint sets to Galton and test Galton's system in his police department.

Galton published a second book on fingerprints, *Finger Print Directories*, in 1895. By then he had subclassified loops according to the number of ridges in them and whorls according to variations in their pattern. This system was an improvement over his first crude one, but Henry and his two Bengali assistants, Azizul (or Azial) Haque and Hemchandra Bose, found that Galton's system, like Bertillon's, was too complicated to teach to most police clerks. They began trying to devise a simpler, more practical classification system.

Henry later recounted in *The Classification and Uses of Finger Prints*, a book he published in 1900, that inspiration for a new fingerprint system struck him during a train journey in late 1896. He had no paper with him, so he wrote his ideas on his shirt cuffs. With Haque and Bose (who, according to some sources, did most of the work), Henry continued to develop this system in early 1897. It took some features from Galton's classification but made the distinctions between types of prints easier to recognize.

What came to be known as the Henry system used the prints of all 10 fingers. Each finger was given a position number, beginning with 1 for the right thumb and ending with 10 for the left little finger. Each print was classified simply as a whorl (W) or a loop (L; arches were counted as loops), a distinction that anyone could make quickly. Each whorl was assigned a numeric value, which depended on the position of the finger on which the whorl appeared (but was not the same as the position number). The assigned values of all the fingers with whorls that occupied even-numbered positions were added together, 1 was added to this total, and the result was written as a single number. Similar treatment of the odd-numbered fingers containing whorls produced a second number. The first number was written above or to the left of the second, separated by a line or slash, producing a figure that looked like (but was not) a fraction. The system had 1,024 potential divisions.

Fingerprinting Takes Over

Henry's fingerprint classification system impressed his superiors because it seemed so much easier to use than the awkward Bertillon system. In mid-1897, the governor-general of India directed that identification of criminals through fingerprints be adopted throughout the country.

THE HENRY SYSTEM

Fingerprint patterns (example):

	Thumb	Index	Middle	Ring	Little
RIGHT HAND	---	---	---	---	---
Finger number	1	2	3	4	5
Finger pattern	Loop	Loop	Arch	Whorl	Loop
LEFT HAND	---	---	---	---	---
Finger number	6	7	8	9	10
Finger pattern	Whorl	Loop	Whorl	Loop	Loop

Henry classification values:

	Thumb	Index	Middle	Ring	Little
Finger number	1	2	3	4	5
Finger pattern	Loop	Loop	Arch	Whorl	Loop
Finger value	16	16	8	8	4
Finger number	6	7	8	9	10
Finger pattern	Whorl	Loop	Whorl	Loop	Loop
Finger value	4	2	2	1	1

© Infobase Publishing

The Henry system of fingerprint classification focuses on fingers that contain whorls. A sample set of 10 fingerprints is shown in the top chart. The bottom chart shows the numeric value that is given to each print in the sample. In the British form of the system, shown here, the classifier adds up the values of all even-numbered fingers that contain whorls, plus 1. Here the sum is 15, because whorls appear in finger number 4 (value = 8), 6 (value = 4), and 8 (value = 2). A second number is obtained by adding the values of the odd-numbered fingers that contain whorls, plus 1. No odd-numbered fingers have whorls in this example, so the second number is simply 1. The two numbers are written like a fraction, with the first number over the second one; in this case, the Henry number is 15/1. In the United States version of the system, the top number is the sum of the values of all the fingers with whorls in the right hand, plus 1. The bottom number is the sum of the values of all the fingers with whorls in the left hand, plus 1.

Word of the new system soon spread to Britain, and Henry's book on fingerprinting was widely read. Henry was appointed assistant commissioner of Scotland Yard (the London metropolitan police force) and head of the Yard's criminal investigation department (CID), or detective branch, in May 1901 and given the task of establishing a fingerprint bureau within the CID.

The fingerprint bureau opened on July 1, 1901. It made 1,722 identifications of repeat criminals in 1902, almost four times as many as anthropometry had done in its best year. "The results obtained appear to fully demonstrate the greater effectiveness as a means of establishing recognitions of the new system, . . . [which] brought about a marked saving of the time of police officers," Scotland Yard reported.

Henry's fingerprint bureau achieved a second victory in 1902, when Harry Jackson was found guilty of burglary on the basis of a thumbprint he had left on the windowsill of a burgled house. This was the first time a fingerprint had helped to convict a criminal in a British court. Fingerprint evidence was first used in a British murder case in May 1905, when a jury convicted two brothers, Alfred and Albert Stratton, of robbing and murdering a paint shop owner and his wife. Alfred Stratton had left a bloody thumbprint on a cashbox at the crime scene.

By this time, police in most other European countries had set up their own fingerprint departments. New York became the first U.S. state to use fingerprints for identification of prisoners in 1903. Several other states, Canada, and the newly established U.S. National Bureau of Identification abandoned anthropometry and adopted fingerprinting during the next several years. Most of these countries and states used the Henry system, which is the basis of most modern fingerprint classification systems.

Francis Galton stopped studying fingerprints soon after the publication of *Finger Print Directories*. He had always cared about fingerprints mainly as a possible tool for studying human heredity, and when he failed to find connections between the prints and other presumably inherited traits, he lost interest in them. Galton was knighted for his scientific achievements in 1909 and died in 1911.

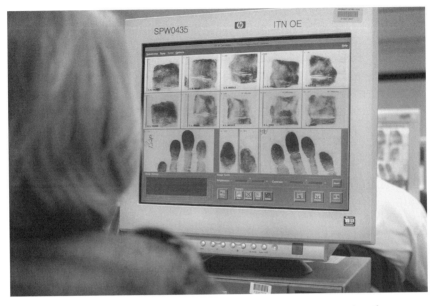

Fingerprint analysts today use computer programs to compare prints from crime scenes or suspects with prints of known criminals. The U.S. Federal Bureau of Investigation (FBI) has created a national database of criminals' fingerprints, the Integrated Automatic Fingerprint Identification System (IAFIS), and computer software that allows analysts to compare prints with those entered by state, local, and national agencies throughout the country. (FBI)

Edward Henry was promoted to commissioner (head) of Scotland Yard on March 11, 1903. He was knighted in 1906 and made a baronet in 1918. He died of a heart attack on February 19, 1931.

Fingerprinting Today

Forensic scientists today examine not only fingerprints but also the prints of palms, toes, and foot soles. Some prints at a crime scene may be patent, or legible—easily visible to the naked eye. Others may be impressed, or plastic, appearing as three-dimensional marks in clay, soap, or other soft materials. Most commonly, prints are latent, or hidden, until revealed by chemicals (powders, liquids, or gases) or special lights. Once a print has been revealed, it is usually

---

ISSUES: HOW RELIABLE ARE FINGERPRINTS?

Fingerprints were considered the "gold standard" of forensic proof throughout the 20th century. Critics of fingerprinting say, however, that the days of courts' unquestioning acceptance of fingerprint evidence may soon be over.

Jennifer L. Mnookin, a professor at the University of Virginia School of Law in Charlottesville, is one such critic. She writes in the Fall 2003 issue of *Issues in Science and Technology,* "there has been woefully little careful . . . examination of the key claims made by fingerprint examiners," such as the statement that no two people have identical fingerprints. Mnookin also maintains that there is "no generally agreed-on standard for precisely when to declare a match" between two fingerprints. She and others who distrust fingerprinting especially question identification on the basis of partial or degraded prints, which are often the only ones available at crime scenes.

Defenders of fingerprinting stress that no two people, even identical twins, have ever been found to have exactly the same prints, even though hundreds of millions of prints have been examined. Scientists have learned that fingerprints are shaped by a combination of genes and factors that affect a child while it is still in the womb. Identical twins carry the same genes, but these other factors make their fingerprints differ slightly. In a reply to Mnookin, published in the Winter 2004 issue of the same magazine, Mary Beeton, vice president of the Canadian Identification Society, states, "I believe that the identification philosophy and scientific methodology together create a solid foundation for a reliable and scientifically valid friction ridge [fingerprint] identification process."

either photographed for further study or "lifted" with a rubber tool or sticky tape and transferred to a card. Scientists have developed more than 40 methods of retrieving fingerprints from crime scenes.

Computers now allow millions of fingerprints to be stored and compared automatically. The U.S. Federal Bureau of Investigation (FBI) began computerizing its fingerprint records in the 1980s and established a national database of convicted criminals' fingerprints, the Integrated Automatic Fingerprint Identification System (IAFIS), in 1999. The prints—more than 47 million of them—come from federal, state, and local law-enforcement agencies. These agencies, in turn, can search the national database for prints matching those at crime scenes. If a match is found, the system transmits the subject's name and criminal history.

Fingerprints are widely used for identification even when no wrongdoing is involved. They appear on driver's licenses, military records, and student ID cards. Use of fingerprints or other forms of biometric identification—identification by means of physical features—is also becoming common at secured entrances to buildings and as a replacement for passwords to control access to computers. Francis Galton, Edward Henry, and the other pioneers of fingerprinting established a technology that affects not only criminals and crime victims but also all other members of society.

Chronology

ca. 2000 years ago	Chinese begin using fingerprints as signatures on contracts
1788	German anatomist J. C. Mayer claims that no two people have the same fingerprints
1822	Francis Galton born in Sparkbrook, England
1823	Czech anatomist Jan Evangelista Purkyně divides fingerprints into nine types
1850	Edward Richard Henry born in Shadwell, Wapping, London, on July 26
1853	Galton wins gold medal from Royal Geographic Society
1858	In July, William Herschel makes road contractor in Bengal, India, sign contract with palm print to keep the man from denying his signature
1860s, 1870s	Herschel encourages use of fingerprints in place of written signatures to prevent fraud; he collects and studies fingerprints

1869	Galton publishes *Hereditary Genius*
	Henry graduates from University College, London
1873	Henry enters civil service of India
1877	As magistrate of Hooghly, Herschel requires fingerprint signatures on all pensions, deeds, and jail warrants
1878	Herschel retires and returns to England
	Henry Faulds, Scottish physician and missionary in Japan, begins collecting and studying fingerprints
1880	Faulds uses fingerprints to identify criminals who committed several local thefts; he writes a letter, published in October 28 issue of *Nature*, that recommends using fingerprints to solve crimes and identify criminals
	Herschel replies to Faulds's letter in the November 25 issue of *Nature*, describing his own earlier work with fingerprinting
1884	Paris police begin using Alphonse Bertillon's anthropometry identification system and identify 241 repeat criminals
	Galton begins studying anthropometry in hope of identifying physical markers inherited with certain mental characteristics
1885	French national prison system adopts anthropometry
1887	Police forces in the United States and Canada begin using anthropometry
1888	Galton writes to Herschel on March 1 to obtain more information about fingerprints
1888–92	Galton collects and studies fingerprints and develops a system for classifying them
1891	Henry becomes inspector-general of police in Bengal in April
1892	Galton publishes *Finger Prints*
	Herschel sends Galton's book to Henry Cotton, chief secretary to the government of Bengal; Cotton passes it on to heads of departments, including Edward Henry

1894	Henry begins working with Galton on fingerprints
1895	Galton publishes *Finger Print Directories,* which includes an improved classification system
1896–97	With Azizul (Azial) Haque and Hemchandra Bose, Henry develops the Henry system of fingerprint classification
1897	In midyear, the governor-general of India directs that identification of criminals through fingerprints be adopted throughout the country
1900	Henry publishes *The Classification and Uses of Finger Prints*
1901	Henry made assistant commissioner of Scotland Yard (London police force) and head of its criminal investigation department (CID) in May CID's fingerprint bureau opens on July 1
1902	CID fingerprint bureau identifies 1,722 repeat criminals Fingerprint evidence convicts first criminal (a burglar) in a British court case
1903	New York becomes first U.S. state to use fingerprints for identification of prisoners Henry becomes commissioner of Scotland Yard on March 11
1903–10	Fingerprinting (usually classified by Henry system) replaces anthropometry for identifying criminals in most European countries, Canada, and U.S. states
1905	Fingerprint evidence convicts brothers Alfred and Albert Stratton of murder in May, the first time such evidence is used in a British murder case
1906	Henry is knighted
1909	Galton is knighted
1911	Galton dies
1918	Henry is made a baronet
1931	Henry dies of a heart attack on February 19

1999   U.S. Federal Bureau of Investigation establishes Integrated Automatic Fingerprint Identification System (IAFIS), a computerized national fingerprint database

Further Reading

Books

Beavan, Colin. *Fingerprints: The Origin of Crime Detection and the Murder Case That Launched Forensic Science*. New York: Hyperion, 2001.
> Book describing the origin of fingerprinting stresses the importance of Henry Faulds's role.

Cole, Simon A. *Suspect Identities: A History of Fingerprinting and Criminal Identification*. Cambridge, Mass.: Harvard University Press, 2001.
> Recounts the development of fingerprinting and other forms of identification, emphasizing governments' use of these methods to keep track of growing numbers of citizens.

Fridell, Ron. *Solving Crimes: Pioneers of Forensic Science*. New York: Franklin Watts, 2000.
> For young adults. Contains chapters on Alphonse Bertillon and Edward Henry.

Galton, Francis. *Finger Print Directories*. London: Macmillan, 1895.
> Includes an improved fingerprint classification system.

———. *Finger Prints*. London: Macmillan, 1892.
> Explains Galton's fingerprint classification system and its use in identification.

———. *Hereditary Genius*. London: Macmillan, 1869.
> Presents Galton's belief that intellectual ability and other mental traits are inherited.

Genge, N. E. *The Forensic Casebook: The Science of Crime Scene Investigation*. New York: Ballantine Books, 2002.
> Contains a chapter describing how modern forensic scientists investigate fingerprints.

Henry, Edward R. *Classification and Uses of Finger Prints*. London: H. M. Stationery Office, 1900.
> Explains the Henry system of classifying fingerprints, developed in India by Henry, Azizul (Azial) Haque, and Hemchandra Bose.

Wilson, Colin, and Damon Wilson. *Written in Blood: A History of Forensic Detection.* New York: Carroll & Graf reissue, 2003.
> Contains a chapter on the development of fingerprinting.

Yeatts, Tabatha. *Forensics: Solving the Crime.* Minneapolis, Minn.: Oliver Press, 2001.
> For young adults. Contains a chapter on fingerprints, stressing the role of Henry Faulds.

Articles

Beeton, Mary, et al. "The Fingerprint Controversy." *Issues in Science and Technology* 20 (Winter 2004): 9–13.
> Several experts comment on Jennifer Mnookin's contention that fingerprint evidence is not reliable.

Faulds, Henry. "Skin Furrows of the Hand." *Nature* 22 (October 28, 1880): 605.
> First published account of the use of fingerprints for identification and first suggestion that fingerprints could be used to tie suspects to crime scenes.

Federal Bureau of Investigation. "IAFIS: Integrated Automated Fingerprint Identification System." Available online. URL: http://www.fbi.gov/hq/cjisd/iafis.htm. Accessed on October 27, 2005.
> Briefly describes features of this national fingerprint database and the services it provides to state and local law-enforcement agencies.

Herschel, William. "Skin Furrows of the Hand." *Nature* 23 (November 25, 1880): 76.
> Herschel's reply to Faulds, describing his own experience with fingerprinting in India beginning in 1858.

Keogh, Eamonn. "An Overview of the Science of Fingerprints." *Anil Aggrawal's Internet Journal of Forensic Medicine and Toxicology* 2 (January–June 2001). Available online. URL: http://www.geradts.com/anil/ij/vol_002_no_001/papers/paper005.html. Accessed on August 6, 2006.
> Describes and illustrates fingerprint classification systems, including the Henry system.

Mnookin, Jennifer L. "Fingerprints: Not a Gold Standard." *Issues in Science and Technology* 20 (Fall 2003): 47–54.
> Criticizes accuracy of fingerprints as forensic evidence and raises general questions about the validity of expert evidence in court.

Ramsland, Katherine. "Fingerprints and Other Impressions." Available online. URL: http://www.crimelibrary.com/criminal_mind/forensics/fingerprints/1.html. Accessed on October 30, 2005.

> Series of 10 articles, part of Court TV's Crime Library, that describes the history of fingerprinting, fingerprinting techniques, and key murder cases that have been solved by fingerprint evidence. The articles also discuss impressions from other body parts, including prints of ears and bare feet.

Tredoux, Gavan. "Henry Faulds: The Invention of a Fingerprinter." Available online. URL: http://galton.org. Posted in December 2003. Accessed on September 24, 2005.

> Criticizes Colin Beavan's claim for the importance of Henry Faulds in *Fingerprints* and stresses Francis Galton's significance in the development of forensic fingerprinting.

Web Sites

Latent Print Reference Grail. CLPEX.com. URL: http://www.clpex.com/Reference.htm. Accessed on September 22, 2005.

> Includes links to numerous articles about fingerprints, including history of fingerprinting; methods of examination; evaluation of fingerprints as evidence; and scientific, ethical, and legal issues brought up by fingerprinting.

Sir Francis Galton F.R.S. 1822–1911. URL: http://galton.org. Accessed on October 23, 2005.

> This site, devoted to Galton, presents overviews of his work in his major areas of interest. It also contains a time line of Galton's life, photographs and portraits, all of his published writings, the complete text of his autobiography and a biography of Galton by Karl Pearson, and contemporary comments on Galton's ideas. It reprints historic works on fingerprinting by Henry Faulds, William Herschel, and Edward Henry as well.

THE LANGUAGE OF BLOOD

KARL LANDSTEINER AND BLOOD TYPES

In William Shakespeare's famous tragedy *Macbeth*, images of blood haunt Lady Macbeth after she and her husband arrange the murder of King Duncan, a guest in their home. Over and over, she tries to wash her hands of bloodstains that only she can see. Many other authors have also used blood as a symbol of murder or violent crime. Only in the 20th century, however, have forensic scientists learned how to read in detail the stories blood can tell. The chief translator of the language of blood was Karl Landsteiner, an Austrian physician and medical researcher.

A Risky Procedure

Karl Otto Landsteiner, born in Vienna, Austria, on June 14, 1868, was the only child of Leopold Landsteiner, a well-known journalist and newspaper publisher. Leopold Landsteiner died suddenly when Karl was only six years old, and Karl's mother, the former Fanny Hess, raised him.

Karl Landsteiner earned his medical degree from the University of Vienna in 1891. He decided to do scientific research rather than treat patients. After five years of additional study at various universities, he began working at the Vienna Pathological Institute in 1898. (Pathology is the study of diseased parts of the body.)

He stayed there for 10 years, then became director of the laboratories at the Royal Imperial Wilhelmina Hospital in Vienna in 1908. He also became a professor of pathological anatomy at the University of Vienna in 1911.

Landsteiner began focusing on serology—the study of blood and other bodily fluids, including saliva, tears, mucus, sweat, and semen—around 1897. He wanted to know what part these fluids played in immunity, the chemical reactions through which the body defends itself against microorganisms that might cause disease. He also hoped to explain a long-standing mystery: why transfusions, or transfers of blood from one human or animal to another, sometimes succeeded and sometimes failed.

Austrian physician and researcher Karl Landsteiner showed in 1901 that humans could be classified into several groups on the basis of differences in their blood. His discovery helped to make safe blood transfusions possible and also gave forensic scientists a way to identify people who left blood at crime scenes. (Albert and Mary Lasker Foundation)

Humans have always understood that blood is essential to life. If even a fraction of the 10 pints (4.7 L) of blood in the average human body is lost, a person may become faint and feel ill. Major blood loss causes death. When someone has lost a large amount of blood, therefore, replacing the missing fluid with blood from another human or, perhaps, even an animal seems an obvious way to save the person's life.

A few early physicians tried to perform transfusions. Jean-Baptiste Denis, a French doctor, gave the first-known blood transfusion to a human (using blood from a lamb) in 1667. British physician James Blundell experimented with human-to-human transfusions in the early 1800s. Some of these doctors' patients survived, but others died. Most physicians concluded that transfusions were too risky to use.

Clues to a Puzzle

Two earlier scientists' work gave Landsteiner clues about why transfusions were sometimes deadly. Leonard Landois, a German researcher, had shown in 1875 that when red blood cells from one species of animal were mixed with serum from another species, the cells stuck together, forming clumps. (Red cells are the cells in the blood that contain hemoglobin, the substance that gives blood its color and carries oxygen throughout the body. Serum, a yellowish fluid, is the liquid part of the blood.) The reaction Landois observed was different from clotting, the normal thickening of blood that stops bleeding from small wounds. Landois found that the clumping also occurred when blood from animals was mixed with that of humans. He realized that if this reaction took place in a living body, the clumping would destroy the red cells and block tiny blood vessels, probably producing severe illness or death. This, he suspected, was what happened in transfusions that failed.

The second researcher, Belgian scientist Jules Bordet, demonstrated 20 years after Landois's discovery that the clumping Landois had seen was an immune reaction. In such a reaction, substances in the serum attach themselves to proteins in the blood that the body identifies as not belonging to it. These serum compounds act as markers, signaling the immune system to destroy the marked proteins and whatever carries them. In the reactions Bordet studied, the damaged proteins settled out of the serum as a white solid, or precipitate, so he called the attacking substances precipitins. (They are now known as antibodies.)

When the "foreign" proteins destroyed by the immune system were on the surfaces of bacteria or viruses, the immune reaction served the body well by killing the invading microorganisms and preventing disease. If the proteins were on red blood cells given in a transfusion, on the other hand, the reaction canceled any helpful effect that the transfusion might have had. For Landsteiner, one question remained: Why did immune reactions ruin some transfusions but not others?

Four Types of Blood

Karl Landsteiner's first research on blood reactions confirmed Landois's observation that clumping took place when serum and cells from two animal species, or from a human and an animal, were mixed. Then, in a breakthrough experiment, Landsteiner went on to show that mixing serum from one human being with red cells from another sometimes produced the same kind of reaction. Landsteiner's tests used only blood from healthy people, so he concluded that the reaction was not due to disease.

Landsteiner mentioned this discovery in a footnote attached to a paper published in 1900, then described it in more detail in a second paper in 1901. In this second paper, he listed three types, or groups, of human blood. He wrote that red cells in blood from people in the first group, type A, carry a certain kind of protein, now called an antigen, on their surfaces. Cells from people with type B, the second group, carry a different antigen. The cells of people with the third type do not contain either antigen. Landsteiner called this third group type C, but today it is known as type O.

Landsteiner's discovery showed clearly why some human-to-human transfusions succeeded and others did not. An individual's serum normally contains precipitins (antibodies) that produce an immune reaction only against the antigen or antigens that the person's own red cells do not carry. Transfusions between two people with the same blood type will usually be safe, Landsteiner concluded, because the cells of both people will contain the same antigen, and their serum will not react to it. If a transfusion takes place between someone with blood type A and a person with type B, on the other hand, clumping will occur because antibodies in the recipient's serum will attack the cells in the donor blood, which carry a "foreign" antigen.

Cells from type O people will not be harmed by serum from either type A or type B people because the cells do not possess either of the antigens that trigger the reaction. (Type O has been called the "universal donor" because blood of this type can be given safely to anyone.) Serum from type O people, on the other hand, will attack both type A and type B blood cells, so people with type O blood can receive transfusions only from other people with type O. In 1902, two of Landsteiner's coworkers rounded out this picture by identifying a fourth blood type, AB, in which some red cells carry the A antigen and others have the B antigen. AB people can safely receive blood from anyone but can donate only to other people with type AB.

By 1907, Landsteiner had worked out a simple test for determining whether a blood transfusion between any two people would be safe. In this test, a technician takes a small sample of cells from a potential blood donor and a sample of serum from an intended recipient. The technician combines cells and serum in a dimple or well on a microscope slide, then looks at the slide under a microscope to see whether the cells clump. Reuben Ottenberg, a surgeon, performed the first successful transfusion based on blood group testing later that same year at Mt. Sinai Hospital in New York.

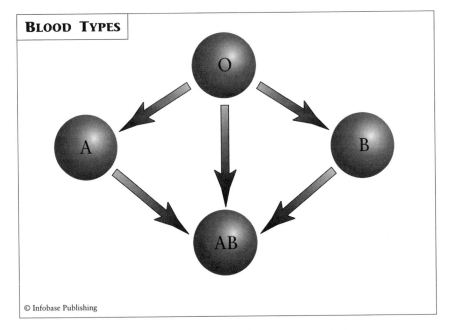

BLOOD TYPES

© Infobase Publishing

Landsteiner and his coworkers discovered that each person belongs to one of four main blood types or groups: A, B, AB, or O. Anyone can safely give blood to or receive blood from anyone else belonging to the same group. People belonging to group O can give blood to anyone but can receive blood only from other type O people. People of types A and B can give blood to people of type AB but not to each other. People of type AB can receive blood from anyone but can give it only to other type AB people.

Most physicians ignored Landsteiner's potentially lifesaving discovery, probably because no one had yet found a way to preserve blood. Blood clots almost instantly after being removed from the body, so it could not be stored. When someone was bleeding to death, doctors seldom had time to locate a potential donor, check the donor's and recipient's blood with Landsteiner's test, and transfuse the blood directly through a tube. Transfusions therefore remained impractical until 1914, when several scientists independently discovered that adding a chemical called sodium citrate to blood would preserve the blood for about 10 days. Preserved blood saved soldiers' lives during World War I, which began in that year, but transfusions were not used on a large scale until the 1930s, when blood preservation was improved further.

In 1901, the same year in which Karl Landsteiner described blood types, German chemist Paul Uhlenhuth invented a test that could show whether a bloodstain had come from a human or an animal. (National Library of Medicine, photo B025272)

Testing Blood to Solve Crimes

Using blood typing to solve crimes was not Karl Landsteiner's main interest, but he recognized that such a use was possible. In a lecture that he gave in 1902 with Max Richter, a professor at the Vienna University Institute of Forensic Medicine, Landsteiner showed how to identify blood groups in dried bloodstains found at crime scenes.

Blood typing could not provide certain identification of a victim or an attacker, Landsteiner and Richter pointed out, because many people have the same blood type. (Landsteiner and others later

---

CONNECTIONS: BLOOD TRANSFUSIONS IN WORLD WAR II

Blood transfusions were not used extensively during World War I because blood treated with sodium citrate alone could not be preserved long enough to be sent easily to war zones. Battlefield surgeons also usually lacked the time and equipment to do blood-typing tests.

By the time World War II started in Europe in 1939, the situation was different. Sergei Yudin, a Russian scientist, had discovered in 1933 that refrigerating blood already treated with sodium citrate allowed the blood to be kept for a month or two. In 1937, Chicago physician Bernard Fantus used this method of preservation to create what he called a blood bank. Blood from donors was typed ahead of time and stored in the bank's refrigerators, ready to use when needed.

Many blood banks were soon established, following Fantus's model. The banks also stored plasma, a liquid made from whole blood by removing all the blood cells. (Plasma is serum plus substances that make blood clot.) Plasma could be used in place of whole blood for many purposes, and it did not require typing. It could also be dried for easy shipping, then made into a liquid once more by adding water.

---

determined that about 40 percent of people have type A blood, 15 percent have type B, 40 percent have type 0, and 5 percent have type AB.) Typing could eliminate some possibilities, however. If a bloodstain on a suspect's clothes was found to be of a different type than that of the crime victim, for instance, that blood could not have come from the victim.

At the same time Landsteiner was doing his key research on blood groups, German chemist Paul Uhlenhuth developed a second blood test that would prove important to forensic science. Chemical tests of the day could show whether a stain at a crime scene contained hemoglobin and therefore was blood, but police had no way to determine whether the blood in the stain came from a human or an animal. Uhlenhuth's test solved this problem.

German planes bombed British cities in the early days of the war, producing many injuries. The United States, not yet at war itself but wanting to help Britain, began a program called "Blood for Britain" in June 1940. During the five months of its operation, the program shipped more than 17,000 pints (7,990 L) of plasma to the beleaguered country. American plasma saved British lives until Britain could set up its own blood banks.

Charles Richard Drew, a young African-American surgeon, headed the Blood for Britain program. He set up a system for collecting blood from volunteers, extracting plasma from it, and storing and shipping the plasma. He made sure that all the blood banks contributing to the program met strict safety standards. When the United States started preparing for its own likely entry into the war shortly afterward, Drew became medical director of the donation program that the armed forces asked the American Red Cross to establish.

During World War II, blood collection drives in the United States brought in more than 13,000,000 pints (6,110,000 L) of blood. Blood from people with group O, the "universal donor" type, was kept as whole blood, and blood from all other groups was made into plasma. Partly because of the new availability of blood and plasma, the death rate among wounded soldiers in World War II was less than half of the death rate in World War I.

Drawing on the work of Bordet and other scientists who had studied immunity, Uhlenhuth, an assistant professor at the Institute of Hygiene in Greifswald, injected small amounts of human blood into rabbits. The rabbits' serum reacted to this foreign blood by creating precipitins (antibodies) that would make human blood cells clump. Uhlenhuth then took serum from the rabbits and mixed it in a test tube with blood from a bloodstain, dissolved in saltwater. If the blood was human, the clumping would make the mixture appear cloudy.

Uhlenhuth first described his invention, which came to be known as the precipitin test or (rather unfairly) the Bordet test, on February 7, 1901. Just a few months later, at the end of July, police asked Uhlenhuth to examine stains on the clothing of Ludwig Tessnow, a German carpenter who was suspected of murdering two little boys as well as mutilating and slaughtering several sheep. Tessnow claimed that the stains came from a wood dye that he used in his work. After examining more than 100 stains on Tessnow's clothes, however, Uhlenhuth showed that some of the stains were human blood, while others came from the blood of sheep. Primarily because of this evidence, Tessnow was found guilty of the boys' murder and sentenced to death.

Most forensic scientists apparently paid little attention to Landsteiner's and Uhlenhuth's discoveries at first, but around 1915, Leone Lattes, a professor of forensic medicine in Turin, Italy, began systematically using blood type identification to solve crimes. Lattes developed a simple test that could determine blood type from only a few flakes of blood or from stains that were up to three months old. Lattes published *The Individuality of Blood,* the first major book about forensic serology, in 1922. By this time, he had improved his test to the point that it could work with bloodstains up to 18 months old.

Thanks largely to Lattes's work, Landsteiner's and Uhlenhuth's tests finally began to be used widely in the late 1920s. Forensic scientists of the period were also impressed to learn that in 80 to 85 percent of people, the proteins that reveal blood type appear not only in blood but also in saliva, semen, and other bodily fluids. This discovery, made in 1925, meant that many kinds of stains found at crime scenes could be examined to determine blood type.

A Delayed Reward

After transfusions and typing of blood at crime scenes began to be used regularly, the scientific world finally recognized Karl Landsteiner's contributions. Landsteiner was awarded the Nobel Prize in physiology or medicine in 1930.

By this time, Landsteiner was living in the United States. Conditions in his native country, Austria, had been so poor after World War I that he felt he could not do research there, so he moved to the Netherlands in 1919. He found life in that country not much better. In 1922, Landsteiner accepted a position at the prestigious

Rockefeller Institute for Medical Research in New York. He became a U.S. citizen in 1929.

Landsteiner continued his research on blood and immune reactions at the Rockefeller Institute, where he remained for the rest of his career. In 1927, he and a coworker, Philip Levine, discovered three more blood-cell antigens, which they named M, N, and P. Landsteiner, a quiet man who preferred studying to socializing and intensely disliked the publicity that came to him in the later part of his life, went on working even after his official retirement in 1939. He and Alexander S. Weiner discovered another major blood antigen, the Rh factor (named for the rhesus monkeys in which it was first detected), in 1940. Landsteiner, in fact, almost died at his workbench: He suffered a heart attack in his laboratory on June 24, 1943, and died two days later.

"Blood Fingerprints"

Researchers found many new types of blood-cell antigens in the 1940s, 1950s, and 1960s. These discoveries helped forensic serologists build up increasingly complex profiles of individuals' blood. Analysts could therefore say with more and more certainty whether the blood in a stain came from a particular person. Some forensic serologists even began to speak of "blood fingerprints." The evidence that no two people could have the same blood profiles was much less strong than evidence for the uniqueness of fingerprints, however. Only DNA testing, developed in the late 1980s, would provide a way of drawing true individual identifications from blood.

Crime scene investigators and forensic serologists today employ tests descended from those developed by Landsteiner, Uhlenhuth, and other pioneers, as well as others created more recently. The Kastle-Meyer test, the modern version of 19th-century chemical tests for hemoglobin, uses a compound called phenolphthalein, which turns bright pink when hemoglobin is present. Detectives reveal hidden bloodstains with Luminol, a spray that makes the stains give off a faint glow in ultraviolet light. A modern version of Uhlenhuth's precipitin test is often used to determine whether the blood in a stain is human or animal, and, if the latter, what kind

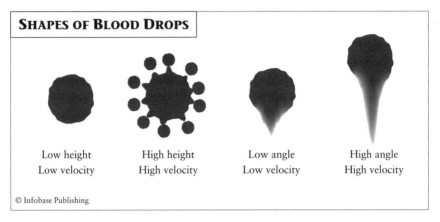

SHAPES OF BLOOD DROPS

| Low height | High height | Low angle | High angle |
| Low velocity | High velocity | Low velocity | High velocity |

© Infobase Publishing

The shape of a blood drop left at a crime scene depends on the height from which it falls, the angle at which it lands, and the speed at which it is moving. The shape of the drops on the right shows that the spatter was moving downward.

of animal. Blood typing and other tests based on immune reactions can give some idea of the age, sex, and race of the person from whom a blood sample came, although this information now would be more likely to come from DNA identification.

Spatter Tells a Story

Blood at a crime scene can reveal more than the possible identity of the person or persons who left the blood behind. Crime scene investigators carefully photograph every surface on which blood appears, adding rulers to show scale. Forensic analysts then use these photographs to determine the size and shape of the blood drops or smears, their location, and the distance between them. Analysis of blood spatter patterns provides clues about the type of weapon used, the number of blows or shots, the heights of the victim and attacker, and the positions and movement of both during the attack.

The size of the blood drops indicates the speed of the spatter: The smaller the drops, the faster they were moving. This information, in turn, can help detectives decide what caused the blood to spray. A mist of tiny drops (smaller than 0.04 inch, or 1 mm, in diameter) suggests a gunshot or an explosion, for example. Larger drops (0.04–0.16 inch, or 1–4 mm) probably came from a stab wound or a blow with a blunt object. The largest drops (0.16–0.32 inch, or 4–8 mm) most likely were moving at fewer than five feet (1.5 m) per second and resulted from the blows of a fist or a small weapon.

Blood drops' shape reveals the distance and direction of the spatter. Drops falling onto a smooth surface from directly overhead are likely to be round. However, if the drops fall from a considerable height, a "crown" of smaller droplets may surround each drop because the original drop bounced up and then fell again, scattering the second time.

If a drop hits the surface at an angle, the leading edge of the drop—the part that hits first—will be round, while the rest will be stretched out and irregular. An analyst will realize that the blood was moving in the direction of the irregular part. A simple mathematical formula uses the drop's width and length to determine the exact angle at which it struck the surface: The longer the droplet, the lower the angle of impact. Determining the angles for a number of drops can lead the investigator back to the point from which the blood came, giving an idea of the positions of the victim and attacker.

Spatter analysis can become extremely complicated because blood may be shed not only from the actual impact of blows but also from the weapons, clothing, or moving bodies of the victim or attacker. Each of these things produces its own pattern of stains. Different types of surfaces also cause different changes in the shape and pattern of blood drops landing on them. Interpreting the language of blood, including its pattern of staining as well as the chemistry that Karl Landsteiner investigated, is as much an art as a science.

Chronology

1667	French physician Jean-Baptiste Denis transfuses the blood of a lamb into a human
1800s	Early in the century, James Blundell, a British physician, experiments with blood transfusions between humans

1868	Karl Otto Landsteiner born in Vienna, Austria, on June 14
1875	German scientist Leonard Landois shows that when serum from one animal species is mixed with red blood cells from another species, the cells clump together and are damaged
1891	Landsteiner earns medical degree from University of Vienna
1895	Jules Bordet, a Belgian researcher, shows that the clumping Landois observed is an immune reaction
1897	Landsteiner begins studying serology and immunity
1898	Landsteiner begins working at the Vienna Pathological Institute
1900	Landsteiner states that mixing serum and red cells from two humans sometimes causes the clumping that Landois and Bordet saw
1901	Landsteiner writes paper describing three blood groups and explaining why mixing blood from some combinations of groups produces clumping, while other combinations do not
	On February 7, Paul Uhlenhuth announces development of a precipitin (antibody) test that can show whether blood in a stain is human; in late July, he uses the test to connect Ludwig Tessnow, a German carpenter, with the murder of two little boys
1902	Landsteiner's coworkers discover a fourth blood group (AB)
	Landsteiner and Max Richter give a lecture in which they show how to identify blood groups in dried bloodstains left at crime scenes
1907	Landsteiner devises a simple test to determine whether a blood transfusion will be safe
	Reuben Ottenberg of Mt. Sinai Hospital in New York performs first successful transfusion based on Landsteiner's test
1908	Landsteiner becomes director of laboratories at Royal Imperial Wilhelmina Hospital in Vienna

1911	Landsteiner becomes professor of pathological anatomy at University of Vienna
1914	Several scientists discover that adding sodium citrate to blood will preserve the blood for about 10 days World War I begins on August 1
1915	Leone Lattes begins using blood-typing tests to solve crimes
1919	Landsteiner moves to the Netherlands
1922	Lattes publishes *The Individuality of Blood* Landsteiner begins working at the Rockefeller Institute for Medical Research in New York
1925	Scientists discover that, in most people, blood type can be identified by testing saliva, semen, and other bodily fluids as well as blood
1927	Landsteiner and Philip Levine discover M, N, and P blood types
1929	Landsteiner becomes U.S. citizen
1930	Landsteiner wins the Nobel Prize in physiology or medicine
1933	Sergei Yudin discovers that if blood is refrigerated as well as treated with sodium citrate, the blood can be preserved for a month or two
1937	Bernard Fantus establishes the first blood bank
1939	Landsteiner officially retires but keeps on working World War II begins in Europe
1940	Landsteiner and Alexander S. Weiner discover Rh factor The United States sends blood plasma to Britain between June and October
1941–45	Donated blood and blood plasma help to reduce the death rate among wounded soldiers to less than half of what it had been in World War I
1943	Landsteiner suffers a heart attack in his laboratory on June 24 and dies on June 26

Further Reading

Books

Evans, Colin. *Murder 2: The Second Casebook of Forensic Detection.* Hoboken, N.J.: Wiley, 2004.
Includes short chapters on serology and blood spatter analysis.
Fridell, Ron. *Solving Crimes: Pioneers of Forensic Science.* New York: Franklin Watts, 2000.
For young adults. Includes a chapter on Landsteiner.
Genge, N. E. *The Forensic Casebook: The Science of Crime Scene Investigation.* New York: Ballantine Books, 2002.
Includes part of a chapter on blood spatter analysis.
Wilson, Colin, and Damon Wilson. *Written in Blood: A History of Forensic Detection.* New York: Carroll & Graf reissue, 2003.
Contains a chapter on blood analysis, including famous murder cases in which such analysis played a major part.
Yount, Lisa. *Milestones in Discovery and Invention: Medical Technology.* New York: Facts On File, 1998.
For young adults. Contains a chapter on Landsteiner and his discoveries. The chapter also describes blood banking and the use of blood transfusions and plasma during World War II.

Articles

"Karl Landsteiner—Biography." In *Nobel Lectures, Physiology or Medicine, 1922–1941.* Available online. URL: http://nobelprize.org/nobel_prizes/medicine/laureates/1930/landsteiner-bio.html. Accessed on January 4, 2006.
Short biography of Landsteiner, published when he won the Nobel Prize in physiology or medicine in 1930.
"Karl (Otto) Landsteiner." In *Contemporary Authors Online.* Farmington Hills, Mich.: Gale Group, 2003.
Brief biographical sketch of Landsteiner covering his career and awards.
Landsteiner, Karl. "Über Agglutinationserscheinungen normalen menschlichen Blutes (On agglutination phenomena of normal human blood)." *Wien. Klin. Wochenschr.* 14 (1901): 1,132–1,134.
Paper in which Landsteiner first described blood groups.

————. "Zur Kenntnis der antifermentativen, lytischen und aggluti-
nierenden Wirkungen des Blutserums und der Lymphe." *Zentbl.
Bakt.* 27 (1900): 357–362.

Paper in which Landsteiner mentioned in a footnote that mixing
blood from two human beings sometimes produced the same immune
reaction as mixing blood from two species of animals.

Ramsland, Katherine. "Serology: It's in the Blood." Available online.
URL: http://www.crimelibrary.com/criminal%5Fmind/forensics/
serology. Accessed on September 22, 2005.

Series of eight articles, part of Court TV's Crime Library, that discusses serology. The articles describe some famous murder cases that
involved analysis of blood (including some in which analysis produced
unclear or faulty results) and techniques of blood spatter analysis.

EVERY CONTACT
LEAVES A TRACE

ALEXANDRE LACASSAGNE, EDMOND LOCARD, AND
FORENSIC SCIENCE LABORATORIES

A single city in France gave birth to an amazing array of forensic science specialties. Determination of time of death, forensic anthropology (examination of bodies and bones after death), forensic ballistics (the study of guns and bullets used in crimes), blood spatter analysis, the study of trace evidence (dust, hair, fibers, and the like), and even psychological profiling of criminals all owe their start to two men who worked in the city of Lyon: Alexandre Lacassagne and his best student, Edmond Locard. Locard set up the world's first forensic science laboratory in two attic rooms in the Lyon courthouse.

A Careful Investigator

Jean-Alexandre-Eugène Lacassagne had plenty of opportunity to study violence in his first career as a military physician and surgeon in North Africa. Born in 1843 in Cahors, a French town near the foot of the Pyrenees, Lacassagne attended military school in Strasbourg before enlisting. He became interested in medical jurisprudence (forensic medicine) while serving in Tunis and Algiers. He studied gunshot wounds and wrote a paper on using tattoos for identification.

Lacassagne's military service ended in 1878. In that same year, he wrote a textbook on forensic medicine, *Précis de médicine légale* (Summary of forensic medicine), which made his reputation in the field. Because of it, the University of Lyon invited him to become a professor of medical jurisprudence.

During the 1880s, Lacassagne spent many hours in the town mortuary, studying the ways human bodies change after death. He recorded how long after death each change took place. For instance, he observed that the skin on the lower part of a body (that is, the part nearest the ground) develops purplish patches in the first hours after someone dies.

Alexandre Lacassagne, professor of legal medicine at the University of Lyon, laid the foundation for several fields of modern forensic science in the 1880s and 1890s. (National Library of Medicine, photo B017192)

This happens because gravity pulls red blood cells downward after the heart stops pumping blood. This change, which begins about half an hour after death, is called livor mortis or lividity. During the first 10 to 20 hours after death, pressing a finger on a purple spot will make the spot vanish, but after that, the spots become permanent because red coloring matter has leaked from the blood into the skin.

Detectives could use changes like livor mortis to determine how long before a body's discovery death had occurred, Lacassagne told his students. He warned them, however, that the environment affects the time line of alterations after death. Changes occur more quickly in a warm place than in a cold one. Lacassagne also pointed out that changes after death could show more than just time of death. Livor mortis appearing on the upper surface of a body is likely to mean that the body was turned over several hours after the person died, for example.

OTHER SCIENTISTS: HANS GROSS (1847–1915)

Hans Gross was almost as important a founder of forensic science as Lacassagne and Locard. Gross was born in 1847 in Graz, Austria, and studied law at Graz University. He then worked for 30 years as an examining magistrate, traveling from town to town to hear testimony about crimes and pass sentence on captured criminals. In the course of this work, he gained tremendous experience in studying physical evidence to determine guilt or innocence. He became famous for the attention he paid to the details of each case.

Gross summed up his expertise in *System der Kriminalistik*, a book published in 1893 (it was reprinted in English in 1907 as *Criminal Investigation*). The book covered many subjects now recognized as part of forensic science, including examination of trace evidence under the microscope, study of suspicious documents (handwriting analysis), fingerprinting, and serology. Gross's book, the first to provide a systematic approach for using science to solve crimes, became what Colin and Damon Wilson, in *Written in Blood: A History of Forensic Detection,* call "the Bible of crime detection." It introduced the term *criminalistics,* often used as a synonym for forensic science.

After two years as a professor of criminology at the University of Prague (in present-day Czech Republic), Gross returned to the University of Graz, where he became a professor of penal law in 1904. In 1912, he founded the world's first criminological institute at the university. The institute included a museum with exhibits of murder weapons and other souvenirs of famous crimes.

A patriotic man of fiery temper, Gross enlisted to fight in World War I even though he was 67 years old at the time. During the war, he developed a lung infection, which caused his death in 1915.

Two Famous Cases

Two cases that Alexandre Lacassagne solved in 1889 made him famous. In one, he identified a murderer by comparing scratches on two bullets under a microscope. These scratches were made by the spiral grooves (rifling) in the barrel of the gun that fired the bullet, and Lacassagne had found that the pattern of scratches differs from gun to gun. He counted seven grooves on a bullet that had been removed from a murdered man. A test bullet, fired from a gun found under the floorboards in the room of a suspect, showed the same seven grooves, so Lacassagne concluded that this man was the murderer. Lacassagne was probably the first person to carry out this kind of comparison, which became a standard part of forensic ballistics.

In the second case, the more widely publicized of the two, Lacassagne faced the unpleasant task of having to identify a man's badly decomposed body. The naked body was first found in August, in a canvas sack hidden in bushes about 10 miles from Lyon. Nearby, police discovered a large trunk that smelled of rotting flesh. Labels on the trunk showed that it had been sent by train from Paris to the Lyon area at the end of July. Paul Bernard, a former student of Lacassagne's, examined the body soon after it was found and concluded that the man had been strangled, but he could learn nothing else about the crime or the man's identity. The body was then buried.

In Paris, meanwhile, assistant police superintendent Marie-François Goron was looking for a missing man, a bailiff (court attendant) named Toussaint-Augssent Gouffé. Gouffé's brother-in-law reported the bailiff's unexplained absence at about the same time the Lyon police found their unidentified body. When Goron heard about the body, he suspected that it might be Gouffé. He ordered the body exhumed (removed from its grave) and sent to Lacassagne, who was recognized throughout France as a forensic expert.

Lacassagne conducted the kind of investigation that today would be carried out by a forensic anthropologist. After cleaning away the rotting flesh, he examined the corpse's skeleton. A defect in the right knee convinced him that the man must have walked with a limp—which proved to be true of Gouffé. Lacassagne concluded on the basis of the bones that the dead man had been about 50 years old; Gouffé was 49. Lacassagne compared a sample of the corpse's hair and a sample of Gouffé's (taken from his hairbrush) under a microscope and declared that the two samples matched. When Goron and other Paris police came to the Lyon scientist's laboratory to learn the results of his investigation, Lacassagne showed them the skeleton and said, "Messieurs, I present you with Monsieur Gouffé."

Further detective work led Goron to identify Gouffé's murderer as a man named Michel Eyraud. Lacassagne played no part in Eyraud's trial, but Eyraud probably never would have been captured if the forensic scientist had not shown that the decayed body was the missing Gouffé.

In the 1890s, Lacassagne explored other fields that would become standard parts of forensic science. He was the first-known person to analyze the shape and patterns of blood drops spattered at crime scenes, for instance. He also did a detailed psychological examination of Joseph Vacher, who was charged with raping and killing at least 11 young people in southwestern France. Vacher showed signs of insanity, but after interviewing the killer for five months in 1897, Lacassagne concluded that Vacher was merely pretending to be mentally ill, perhaps in hope of a reduced sentence. Lacassagne's

In addition to continuing the work of his teacher, Lacassagne, Edmond Locard set up the world's first forensic science laboratory in Lyon and solved numerous crimes by examining dust and other trace evidence. (Roger-Viollet)

study is thought to be the first in-depth psychological profile of a serial killer. Vacher was convicted of one of the murders in October 1898 and executed two months later.

The First Forensic Science Laboratory

During the years when his research was establishing one forensic field after another, Lacassagne also continued teaching at the University of Lyon. Edmond Locard, one of his students during the 1890s, must have struck him as someone special. After Locard earned doctorates in medicine and law, Lacassagne hired the young man as his assistant. Lacassagne's confidence was well placed: In the opinion of crime historians such as Colin and Damon Wilson, Locard eventually surpassed his teacher as a forensic scientist.

Lacassagne's interest in forensics had been stirred on the battlefield, but Locard's came from books. Locard was born in Lyon in 1877, just a year before Lacassagne's military career ended. As a child, Locard's favorite reading was a French translation of British author Arthur Conan Doyle's stories about a fictional detective, Sherlock Holmes. Holmes used careful observation, logical reasoning, and scientific tests to work out solutions to mysterious crimes. He became the inspiration for Locard's career.

Locard attended a Dominican college in the town of Quillins, then continued his studies at the University of Lyon. He came to see Alexandre Lacassagne, his teacher in forensic medicine at the university, as a real-life hero just as important to him as the fictional Sherlock Holmes. Locard took to heart Lacassagne's often-repeated warning, "One must know how to doubt."

During the first years of the 20th century, in addition to assisting Lacassagne, Locard continued his education by visiting eminent forensic scientists in Paris, Lausanne (Switzerland), Rome, Berlin, Brussels (Belgium), New York, and Chicago. He begged the Lyon police department to let him set up a laboratory where he could examine fingerprints, blood, and other evidence found at crime scenes with the scientific methods he learned from these experts. Police officials were reluctant at first, but in 1910, they finally granted Locard's wish—more or less.

Locard's Laboratoire Interrégionale de Police Technique (Interregional Laboratory of Police Technique) had an impressive name but not much more. It consisted of a mere two rooms on the top floor of the Lyon courthouse. Locard and two assistants made up its staff, and its equipment consisted of a microscope and a spectroscope (a device that could be used to determine the chemical makeup of a sample). Limited as it was, Locard's facility was still a

---

CONNECTIONS: MODERN FORENSIC SCIENCE LABORATORIES

Most modern forensic science laboratories are attached to police departments, just as Edmond Locard's was. Some are connected instead to the office of the district attorney or of the coroner or medical examiner, an official who performs autopsies on people who die under suspicious circumstances. A few laboratories are privately run. Police departments or attorneys hire them when a special type of expertise is needed.

A large city or state forensic science laboratory may employ more than 200 people and work on more than 75,000 cases a year. Such a laboratory is usually divided into several departments. One typical department, the serology division, examines all evidence related to bodily fluids. The laboratory's chemistry or toxicology division looks for drugs, poisons, and other chemicals, while the ballistics division deals with guns, bullets, and tools, including knives. A trace evidence division studies anything small enough to be examined under a microscope, including hair, dust, and fibers. Alternatively, serology and trace evidence from bodies, including DNA, may both be handled by a biology division. Fingerprinting, document examination, and other specialties have their own divisions in some laboratories.

Scientists who work in forensics laboratories usually do not collect physical evidence at crime scenes or interview suspects or witnesses. Instead, crime scene technicians, sometimes called criminalists, gather the evidence and bring it to the laboratory. The scientists analyze the evidence, then report the results to police detectives or district attorneys. Forensic scientists also frequently testify about their findings in court.

groundbreaking achievement: the first laboratory in the world to be dedicated to forensic science.

Telltale Dust

Among the many types of physical evidence found at crime scenes, Locard's special interest was dust and other bits of matter almost too small to see—what today would be called trace evidence. He told police to collect trace evidence the same way an archaeologist would unearth material from an ancient site: layer by layer, keeping material from the different layers separate and carefully noting the order in which the layers were removed.

Dust, Locard wrote in *Traité de criminalistique* (Treatise on criminalistics), "contains distinctive characteristics which permit us to determine its origin." In the decade after setting up his forensic science laboratory, Locard assembled, in effect, a database of dust, consisting of samples of every kind of metal, plant, and other material he could find. He used this collection to help him identify particles within the dust taken from crime scenes. Dust from clothing, he pointed out, could show which objects a suspect had brushed past or touched.

In 1911, Locard solved his first major crime by examining dust from suspects' pockets. Police in Paris were trying to break up a group of counterfeiters, or makers of false money—coins in this case. Detectives had identified several suspects, but they could find no proof that the men had committed the crime. When the detectives came to Locard for help, he asked them to let him see the suspects' clothes. The puzzled officers refused at first, but they finally sent him clothing belonging to one of the men they had questioned.

Locard carefully brushed dust from the garments, especially the sleeves, onto a sheet of white paper. He then examined the dust under a microscope and noticed tiny shavings of metal in it. Chemical tests revealed that these fragments included tin, antimony, and lead, the same metals used in the fake coins. The three metals, furthermore, made up the same proportions in the dust that they did in the coins. Impressed with Locard's discovery, the police gave the Lyon scientist clothing from the other two suspects as well. Locard found the same

PARALLELS: SHERLOCK HOLMES, FICTIONAL FORENSIC SCIENTIST

In the late 19th and early 20th centuries, stories about Sherlock Holmes, surely the best-known fictional detective of all time, introduced the reading public of Europe and North America to the idea of a detective as a scientist who identifies criminals by carefully examining evidence and drawing logical conclusions from it. Alexandre Lacassagne, Edmond Locard, and Hans Gross were spreading that concept among police professionals at the same time.

Sherlock Holmes was the creation of Sir Arthur Conan Doyle (1859–1930), a British writer. Doyle worked at first as a medical doctor but turned increasingly to writing in the late 1880s. His first Holmes story, *A Study in Scarlet,* appeared in 1887 and was an immediate success.

Doyle said that he based the character of Sherlock Holmes on Dr. Joseph Bell, one of Doyle's teachers at the medical school in Edinburgh, Scotland. Bell amazed patients and students alike by using his keen observation to identify illnesses and guess patients' past histories. Doyle was also inspired by the work of U.S. writer Edgar Allan Poe (1809–49), who had composed several stories starring a fictional French detective, Auguste Dupin, beginning with *The Murders in the Rue Morgue* in 1841. Poe's tales are generally held to have been the first detective stories.

In a passage from *A Study in Scarlet,* the story's narrator, Sherlock Holmes's friend Dr. Watson, describes Holmes behaving in a way that Lacassagne, Gross, or Locard—or any modern forensic scientist—would immediately recognize:

> He whipped a tape measure and a large round magnifying glass from his pocket. With these two implements he trotted noiselessly about the room, sometimes stopping, occasionally kneeling, and once lying flat upon his face. So engrossed was he with his occupation that he appeared to have forgotten our presence. . . . For twenty minutes or more he continued his researches, measuring with the most exact care the distance between marks which were entirely invisible to me, and occasionally applying his tape to the walls in an equally incomprehensible manner. In one place he gathered up very carefully a little pile of grey dust from the floor, and packed it away in an envelope. . . .
>
> "They say that genius is an infinite capacity for taking pains," he remarked with a smile. "It's a very bad definition, but it does apply to detective work."

metals in dust from their pockets. His evidence helped to send the three men to prison.

Locard solved a murder case by analyzing trace evidence a year later. A young woman, Marie Latelle, had been found strangled in her home on the outskirts of Lyon. The police suspected the man she had been dating a bank clerk named Émile Gourbin. Gourbin, however, said he had been playing cards with friends all evening, and the friends confirmed his story.

At the police's request, Locard examined Latelle's body. He noticed some places on her throat where the murderer's fingers appeared to have scraped off her skin while gripping her neck. Locard then visited Gourbin and carefully collected material from under the clerk's fingernails. When Locard looked at the scrapings with his microscope, he found flakes of what he recognized as human skin, mixed with several compounds that he identified as ingredients in face powder.

The police found a box of pink face powder in Latelle's bedroom and learned that a local druggist had made the powder especially for her. Analyzing the powder in the box, Locard found exactly the same substances as in the sample from Gourbin's fingernails—and, as with the counterfeiters, in the same proportions. When police confronted Gourbin with this evidence, the clerk confessed that he had strangled Latelle. He said he had prepared an alibi by setting his friends' clock ahead.

Clues to Identity

Identification was another forensic subject that fascinated Locard. "To write the history of identification is to write the history of criminology," he wrote in *Traité de criminalistique*. He wrote a book on methods of demonstrating identity, *Proofs of Identity,* which was published in 1932.

Locard's chief invention in the field of identification was poroscopy, which he considered an improvement on Edward Henry's widely accepted system for classifying fingerprints. With the help of a microscope, Locard counted the minute pores, or openings through which sweat comes, in a small area of a fingerprint. He found that one square inch (6.4 cm²) contains an average of 2,700 pores. He believed that the specific number and arrangement of pores were as dependably individual as the fingerprint itself. Locard claimed that poroscopy could help police match fingerprints in cases where partial prints found at a crime scene were too small to compare with the Henry system.

Locard testified in a burglary case in 1912 that the number of pores in a certain area of a suspect's hand matched the number of pores in the same area of a fingerprint found at the crime scene. He demonstrated the match to the jury by using greatly enlarged photographs of the partial prints. He also used poroscopy to solve several other cases in 1912 and 1913. Police found Locard's painstaking system too hard to apply, and poroscopy never became popular. However, many police departments still follow Locard's recommendation, made in 1918, that 12 points of similarity between two fingerprints be required for the fingerprints to be considered a match.

The Exchange Principle

Locard took Lacassagne's place as professor of forensic medicine at the University of Lyon in the 1920s (Lacassagne died in 1924) and taught a new generation of forensic scientists. He also became the founding director of the university's Lyon Institute of Criminalistics. Locard retired in 1951, but he remained active in forensic science until his death in 1966. His best-known work was his seven-volume book, *Traité de criminalistique* (Treatise on criminalistics), which first appeared in 1912. It went through seven editions and was the basic text for forensic scientists during the first half of the 20th century.

The part of Locard's teachings most remembered today is often called the exchange principle. A criminal, Locard said, is bound to leave something behind at a crime scene, take something away, or both. Material left behind could include fingerprints, tire tracks, threads or scraps of cloth, or hair. Blood droplets or hairs from the victim, dirt or plant matter from an outdoor scene, or fibers from carpets or upholstery are examples of things that might be unknowingly taken away. Locard liked to say, "Every contact leaves a trace."

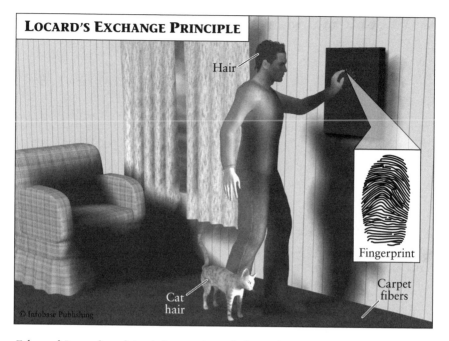

LOCARD'S EXCHANGE PRINCIPLE

Hair

Fingerprint

Carpet fibers

Cat hair

© Infobase Publishing

Edmond Locard explained that a criminal always leaves something at a crime scene and takes something away. Finding those "exchanged" traces can help detectives identify the criminal. In the example shown here, the man burglarizing the wall safe has left his fingerprint on the safe, and a strand of his hair has fallen onto the carpet. At the same time, his pants have picked up fibers from the carpet and fur from the cat that brushed against his leg.

Discovery and analysis of these traces can prove that a suspect was at a crime scene and sometimes provide convincing evidence that he or she committed the crime.

Secrets in Trace Evidence

Forensic scientists of today, like Edmond Locard and Sherlock Holmes, examine every scrap of unusual material found at a crime scene. They collect trace evidence with small vacuum cleaners, tweezers, or lifting tape and place it in envelopes, bottles, or boxes. "If you hear a Dustbuster and see nothing but legs sticking out of a trunk, or some guy picking grains of sand out of floorboards with tweezers, it's probably a trace examiner," trace analyst Jay Paresh told N. E. Genge, author of *The Forensic Casebook.* "They're also the ones with little bottles in their glove compartments, the ones with bottles rattling in their pockets. [They're] compulsive collectors."

After evidence reaches the laboratory, microscopes, spectrometers, and computers become a trace analyst's most important tools. Microscopes reveal details of structure, and spectrometers determine chemical makeup. Computer databases of materials, such as types of paint, fibers, and glass, let analysts identify evidence by matching.

Once identified, trace materials provide many clues about a crime. Paint chips from the site of a hit-and-run accident, for instance, can reveal the make, model, and year of the car that left the scene. Soil and seeds, pollen, or other plant material may show a location from which a victim or a perpetrator came. Fibers can be matched to clothing or upholstery belonging to a suspect.

Trace evidence alone usually cannot prove that a particular person committed a crime. Some fibers, seeds, paint types, and so on are less common than others, but most are likely to exist in more than one place or in objects owned by many people. Trace evidence can be used to pressure a suspect to confess, however, or to make a prosecution (or defense) case more convincing to a jury. In the hands of a careful analyst, trace evidence can tell a powerful story.

Chronology

1841	U.S. author Edgar Allan Poe writes first detective story
1843	Jean-Alexandre-Eugène Lacassagne born in Cahors, France
1877	Edmond Locard born in Lyon, France
1878	Lacassagne's service as a military physician and surgeon in North Africa ends; he publishes *Précis de médicine légale* and becomes professor of medical jurisprudence at University of Lyon

1880s	Lacassagne documents time line of changes after death
1887	Arthur Conan Doyle publishes first Sherlock Holmes story, *A Study in Scarlet*
1889	Lacassagne solves two famous murder cases
1893	Hans Gross publishes *System der Kriminalistik* (reprinted in 1907 as *Criminal Investigation*)
1890s	Lacassagne establishes other fields of forensic science, including blood spatter analysis and psychological profiling
	Locard learns forensic science from Lacassagne; he earns doctorates in medicine and law and becomes Lacassagne's assistant
1897	Lacassagne interviews accused serial killer Joseph Vacher for five months to determine whether Vacher is insane
1900–10	Locard visits eminent forensic scientists in several European cities
1910	Locard sets up world's first forensic science laboratory in Lyon courthouse
1911	Locard identifies counterfeiters by analyzing dust from their clothes
1912	Locard solves a murder by identifying material under the fingernails of a suspect; he solves several cases by counting pores in fingerprints and publishes first edition of *Traité de criminalistique*
1920s	Locard becomes professor of forensic medicine at University of Lyon and founding director of university's Institute of Criminalistics
1924	Lacassagne dies
1932	Locard publishes *Proofs of Identity*
1951	Locard retires
1966	Locard dies

Further Reading

Books

Evans, Colin. *Murder 2: The Second Casebook of Forensic Detection.* Hoboken, N.J.: Wiley, 2004.
> Contains brief biographical profiles of Alexandre Lacassagne, Edmond Locard, and Hans Gross.

Fridell, Ron. *Solving Crimes: Pioneers of Forensic Science.* New York: Franklin Watts, 2000.
> For young adults. Contains a chapter on Edmond Locard.

Genge. N. E. *The Forensic Casebook: The Science of Crime Scene Investigation.* New York: Ballantine Books, 2002.
> Contains material on analysis of trace evidence, including descriptions of cases in which such evidence played a key role.

Gross, Hans. *Criminal Investigation.* New York: Sweet & Maxwell reissue, 1924.
> Gross's handbook for examining magistrates and other investigators of crimes, first issued in 1893, introduces the term *criminalistics* and describes many branches of modern forensic science for the first time.

Locard, Edmond. *Traité de Criminalistique.* 7 vols. 7th ed. Lyon, France: Joannes Desvigne, 1940.
> Locard's most important book, a basic text for forensic scientists for almost half a century. It was first published in 1912.

Wilson, Colin, and Damon Wilson. *Written in Blood: A History of Forensic Detection.* New York: Carroll & Graf reissue, 2003.
> Contains material on Alexandre Lacassagne, Edmond Locard, and their most famous cases.

Articles

Ramsland, Katherine. "Trace Evidence." Available online. URL: http://www.crimelibrary.com/criminal_mind/forensics/trace/1.html. Accessed on November 11, 2005.
> Series of six articles, part of Court TV's crime library, that describes the collection of fibers, hairs, and other trace evidence and cases in which this kind of evidence has been important.

5
THE NAME ON THE BULLET

CALVIN GODDARD AND FIREARMS IDENTIFICATION

When the Chinese invented gunpowder around A.D. 1000, they probably were not thinking of doing a favor to murderers. However, their invention—mostly in the form of bullets fired from handguns (invented in the Middle East about A.D. 1200)—accounted for 70 percent of all murders in the United States in 2004, according to the Federal Bureau of Investigation (FBI).

Fortunately, the designers of handguns have just as unknowingly done a favor to police. Because of the way guns and bullets are manufactured and fired, bullets and the weapons that use them have features as unique as a name or a fingerprint. These features often let analysts who specialize in the study of firearms say precisely which gun fired a particular bullet. Calvin Goddard, a physician who became a gun expert, was a pioneer developer of this branch of forensic science—firearms identification, or forensic ballistics.

From Medicine to Murder

Born on October 30, 1891, in Baltimore, Maryland, Calvin Hooker Goddard began his career as a medical doctor. (His father, Henry Perkins Goddard, was an insurance executive and writer; his mother was Eliza Acheson Goddard.) Goddard earned a B.A. from Johns Hopkins University in Baltimore in 1911 and an M.D. from the uni-

Calvin Goddard solved several famous crimes by examining guns and bullets. He set up the Scientific Crime Detection Laboratory at Northwestern University, near Chicago, in 1930 and helped to found the forensic science specialty of forensic ballistics. (Northwestern University Archives)

versity's medical school in 1915, the same year he married Eliza Harrison. He and his wife later had two daughters.

The year after he became a physician, Goddard enlisted in the U.S. Army and became a first lieutenant in the army medical corps. He served in the United States and Europe until 1920. Between 1920 and 1925, Goddard taught at several universities and worked in private practice as a heart specialist. He also joined the army ordnance (gunnery) reserve.

In 1925, at the age of 34, Goddard decided to change his lifelong interest in guns from a hobby to a full-time career. He joined the Bureau of Forensic Ballistics in New York City, then the country's only laboratory dedicated to the examination of firearms and bullets used in murders and other crimes.

An Unjust Conviction

The Bureau of Forensic Ballistics was founded by Charles E. Waite, an employee of the New York state prosecutor's office. Inspiration for the bureau grew out of a disturbing murder case that Waite reviewed in 1917.

In that case, Charles Stielow, a farmworker, was accused of shooting the farm's owner, Charles Phelps, and Phelps's housekeeper, Margaret Walcott, during a robbery in 1915. Stielow owned a .22-caliber revolver, the same caliber as the bullets taken from Phelps's and Walcott's bodies. (Caliber is the diameter of the inside of a gun barrel, measured in inches. A .22-caliber gun has a barrel diameter of 0.22 inch, or 0.56 cm.) Albert Hamilton, a self-proclaimed gun expert, testified at Stielow's trial that the bullets in the bodies came from the accused man's gun.

Stielow was found guilty of murder and sentenced to death in the electric chair. The deputy warden of the prison to which Stielow was sent had doubts about the verdict, however, and persuaded several wealthy women to hire private detectives to reexamine the case. The detectives learned that two homeless men named King and O'Connell had been seen in the area at the time of the killing. The two were later convicted of theft in a different case and sent to prison.

The women sent attorney Grace Humason to interview King, and he admitted to her that he had murdered Phelps and Walcott. In spite of this, Orleans County, the county in which Stielow had been tried, refused to review Stielow's case or prosecute King. (In *Written in*

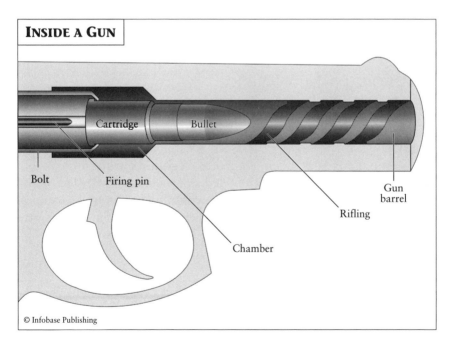

INSIDE A GUN

Cartridge

Bullet

Bolt

Firing pin

Gun barrel

Rifling

Chamber

© Infobase Publishing

This diagram shows the parts of a gun involved in firing. Each part leaves scratches or other marks on the bullet and cartridge casing that forensic ballistics experts can use to identify the gun from which a bullet came.

Blood: A History of Forensic Detection, Colin and Damon Wilson claim that the county did not want to pay for a second trial.) When Stielow's supporters told the governor of New York what had happened, the governor asked attorney George H. Bond and Charles Waite to look into the matter.

Waite, in turn, told several firearms experts in the New York City police department to examine Stielow's revolver again. They found that the barrel of the gun was so clogged with grease and rust that it could not have been fired for years. They also compared photographs of test bullets fired from the revolver and photos of the murder bullets and, contrary to what Hamilton had said, found obvious differences between them. Acting on this evidence, the governor pardoned Stielow, and the farmworker was released—after spending three years in prison for a crime he did not commit.

The Stielow case deeply upset Charles Waite. He never wanted to see another innocent man imprisoned because of the testimony of a false expert like Hamilton. Waite determined to make gun and bullet examination into a reputable science.

Setting up a New Science

Waite first set out to create a catalog of gun and bullet characteristics that he hoped would be as precise as the classifications that police laboratories used for fingerprints. Such a catalog was possible because of the way guns and bullets are made. Beginning in the 1490s, gunsmiths had learned that if they added spiral cuts to the inside of gun barrels, this rifling, as it was called, would make the bullets spin in flight. The spinning, in turn, gave guns the power to send bullets over longer distances and to direct their flight more accurately.

As a bullet passes through a rifled gun barrel, the cuts inside the barrel scratch a unique pattern onto the bullet's surface. Like a fingerprint, the pattern consists of raised ridges alternating with depressions or valleys. In the case of bullets, the ridges are called lands and the depressions are termed grooves. Each type of gun (except for shotguns, the only type of modern gun that is not rifled) leaves its own series of lands and grooves on its bullets. The patterns vary in width, depth, and pitch, or angle.

Beginning around 1918, Waite visited gun manufacturers throughout the United States and asked them to give him the rifling patterns for all their models. Finding that European-made guns were also common in the United States, he added these weapons to his catalog in 1922. He also did research to confirm his belief that, even within a particular model of gun, the rifling in the barrel of each weapon is slightly different because gunmaking machines wear down from gun to gun. Waite claimed that these variations would potentially let analysts identify not only the type of firearm but also the individual gun from which any bullet came.

This gun catalog, exhaustive as it was, was only part of Waite's plan. He also wanted a laboratory devoted to comparing guns and bullets, which police could call on to settle puzzling cases. With two partners, physicist John H. Fisher and chemist Philip O. Gravelle, Waite established the Bureau of Forensic Ballistics for this purpose in New York City in 1923.

During the bureau's first year of operation, Fisher and Gravelle both invented devices that became essential in forensic ballistics. Fisher produced the helixometer, a long, hollow probe with an attached light and magnifying glass that could be used to look into a gun barrel and examine the twist, or helix, of its rifling. Gravelle created the comparison microscope, in which halves of two bullets (one from a crime scene and one test-fired from a suspect's gun) could be viewed as a single image for easy comparison of their markings, or striations.

A Disputed Verdict

Charles Waite died of a heart attack on November 14, 1926, and Calvin Goddard took his place as head of the Bureau of Forensic Ballistics. Goddard traveled around the United States and Europe to demonstrate the bureau's equipment and methods and soon became well known as a firearms expert.

Because of his high reputation, Goddard was asked to give his opinion in one of the most controversial murder cases of the 1920s. The case began on April 15, 1920, when two guards carrying payroll money for a shoe factory were killed during a robbery in South Braintree, Massachusetts. Two Italian immigrants, Nicola Sacco

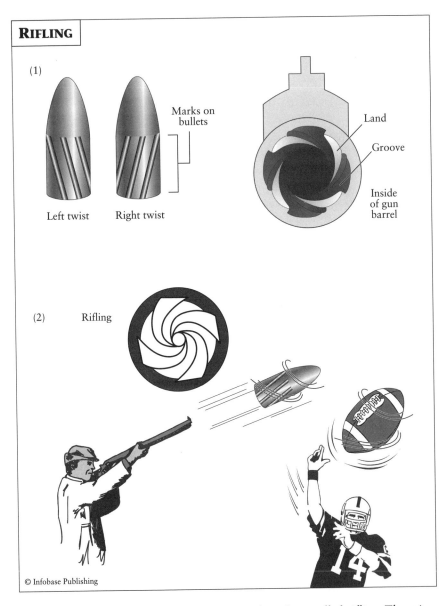

RIFLING

(1)

Marks on bullets

Left twist   Right twist

Land

Groove

Inside of gun barrel

(2)   Rifling

© Infobase Publishing

1. The spiral lines cut into the inside of a gun barrel are called rifling. The spiral may twist to the left or the right. The raised parts of the spiral are lands, and the depressed spaces between the lands are grooves. Different kinds of guns show differences in the direction and angle of rifling and in the width of the lands and grooves. Rifling marks on bullets can be used to identify the guns that fired them. 2. The purpose of rifling is to make a bullet spin, which makes the bullet fly farther and more accurately. A football player throws a football with a spinning motion for the same reason.

and Bartolomeo Vanzetti, were charged with the crime. Both men were anarchists, members of a political group that believed all forms of government are threats to freedom and should be overthrown, by violence if necessary.

Popular feeling against immigrants was high at the time, and dislike of anarchists, who had been blamed for several recent bombings, was even stronger. This feeling extended into the courtroom in Dedham, Massachusetts, where Sacco and Vanzetti's trial began on May 31, 1921: Webster Thayer, the trial judge, was heard to call the defendants "those anarchist bastards." Gun experts for the prosecution and the defense disagreed about whether the bullets taken from the guards' bodies had come from Sacco's revolver. Nonetheless,

The helixometer was invented by physicist John H. Fisher around 1923. The helixometer is a long, hollow probe with an attached light and magnifying glass that could be used to look into a gun barrel and examine the twist, or helix, of its rifling. The helixometer shown here, called a Spencer helixometer, was used at Calvin Goddard's Scientific Crime Detection Laboratory at Northwestern University. (Northwestern University Archives)

the jury convicted both men of the guards' murder on July 14, and Thayer sentenced them to death.

Not everyone was convinced that Sacco and Vanzetti were guilty. Left-wing groups felt that the men's conviction had more to do with dislike of their race and political beliefs than with proof that they had actually committed the crime, and one such organization, Red Aid, raised money for a retrial. The court denied the group's first appeals, but in June 1927, a committee was appointed to review the case. The committee asked Calvin Goddard to reexamine the firearms evidence. Goddard looked at a bullet from the crime scene and a bullet test-fired

---

PARALLELS: TRACKING A SHOOTOUT

Just as Calvin Goddard did with the Sacco-Vanzetti case in the 1920s, a later forensic ballistics expert, Herbert McDonell, had to find out what happened in a highly publicized case with strong political overtones. The events McDonell investigated took place in the early hours of December 4, 1969, when 16 Chicago police officers broke into a house where nine members of the Black Panthers, a radical African-American political group, were staying. During the shootout that followed, two Panthers (including the group's leader, Fred Hampton) were killed and four others were wounded. Police charged the surviving Panthers with attempted murder for firing at them.

The Panthers, like Sacco and Vanzetti and their anarchist companions, made no secret of their willingness to use violence to accomplish their aims. The district attorney for Cook County, in which the shootout took place, stated that the gunfire began when police knocked on the door of a room in which Hampton was sleeping and other Panthers in the room shot at them. The attorney representing the Panthers, on the other hand, claimed that the police had fired first and made a special effort to kill Hampton.

In the Sacco-Vanzetti appeal, Goddard had needed to find out whether the bullets used in the guard's murder came from Sacco's gun. McDonell faced a different forensic task: determining which guns known to be involved in the shootout had fired which bullets, and—most important—finding out which group had shot first.

from Sacco's gun under the forensic ballistics bureau's comparison microscope and concluded that the two matched. The defense's gun experts, taking their turn at the microscope, reluctantly agreed.

Sacco and Vanzetti were executed in the electric chair on August 23, 1927. Questions about their guilt, particularly that of Vanzetti, continue to this day. However, reviews with the most modern forensic ballistics equipment in 1961 and again in 1983 confirmed Goddard's conclusion about the gun. The name of the person who fired the weapon might remain in some doubt, but identification of the weapon itself apparently does not.

McDonell tracked the directions of the bullets' flight by, for example, examining the splintering on door panels through which the bullets had passed. To demonstrate the bullets' flight paths, he pushed straws and metal rods through the holes. Colin and Damon Wilson write that, after a 12-hour investigation of the murder house, McDonell announced that only one shot, a shotgun blast, had come from inside the room in which Hampton was killed. All the rest had come from outside. An informer had told police where Hampton slept before the shootout, and McDonell showed that most of the bullets had been aimed at the spot where Hampton's head was lying.

Using a scale model of the rooms involved in the shootout, McDonell demonstrated during the Panthers' trial that the door to the bedroom was partly shut when one of the police bullets went through it. When the Panthers' shotgun was fired, on the other hand, the door was completely open. The police therefore had to have begun shooting before anyone fired at them.

Attorneys from the opposing side tried to throw doubt on McDonell's testimony, just as had happened with Goddard during the Sacco-Vanzetti trial. However, the FBI later examined the forensic evidence from the Panther shootout and supported McDonell's conclusions. The charges against the seven Panthers were dismissed, and in 1982, a judge ordered Cook County to pay the group $1.85 million in damages for violating their civil rights.

Death on Valentine's Day

A second famous case, in 1929, raised Calvin Goddard's reputation even further. On February 14—Valentine's Day, a holiday usually associated with love rather than violent death—seven members of George "Bugs" Moran's organized crime gang were slaughtered with machine guns in a warehouse in Chicago. Chicago police asked Goddard to help them investigate what came to be known as the St. Valentine's Day Massacre.

Because some of the men whom witnesses saw running away from the warehouse had been wearing police uniforms, the grand jury investigating the gangsters' deaths wanted to know whether police had carried out the execution-style slaying. To find out, Goddard compared bullets from all machine guns belonging to the Chicago police with those recovered from the warehouse. He told the grand jury that none of the murder bullets had come from a police weapon.

Two wealthy Chicagoans on the grand jury were so impressed with Goddard's work that they promised to pay for a forensic science laboratory in the city if Goddard would move to Chicago and set it up. Goddard accepted their offer. He visited forensic science laboratories in 13 European countries during 1929 and 1930 to gain ideas for the new facility.

Goddard opened the Scientific Crime Detection Laboratory in 1930 as part of the school of law at Northwestern University in Evanston, a Chicago suburb. This laboratory, which handled not only ballistics but also serology, toxicology, handwriting analysis, fingerprinting, and examination of trace evidence, was the country's first privately owned comprehensive crime center. Goddard also became a professor of police science at the university.

The Chicago police, meanwhile, continued their search for the shooters in the St. Valentine's Day Massacre. In December 1929, seeking the person who had shot a police officer in a separate event, they raided the home of Fred Burke, a professional killer. Burke had often worked for Al Capone, a gang leader who was a rival of Moran's. The police found a number of weapons at Burke's house, including two Thompson machine guns, the type of weapon that had fired the bullets in the warehouse. Calvin Goddard examined these two guns in 1930 and found that they had been used in the

Chicago killing. Burke was sentenced to life in prison for his role in the shooting.

Return to the Army

Goddard's laboratory inspired many imitations, including the FBI's forensic science laboratory, which was founded in 1932. By the

---

TRENDS: MURDERS BY FIREARMS

FBI statistics show that in recent years firearms have consistently accounted for about 70 percent of all U.S. murders in which the weapon was known. The following table shows the statistics for total murders, firearms of different types, and, for comparison, the next most widely used category of weapons (knives or cutting instruments), for the years between 2000 and 2004.

Weapons	2000	2001	2002	2003	2004
total murders for which weapon is known	12,431	12,816	13,389	13,658	13,265
total murders committed by firearms	8,661	8,890	9,528	9,659	9,326
handguns	6,778	6,931	7,294	7,745	7,265
rifles	411	386	488	392	393
shotguns	485	511	486	454	507
other guns	53	59	75	76	117
firearms, type not stated	934	1,003	1,185	992	1,044
knives or cutting instruments	1,782	1,831	1,776	1,828	1,866

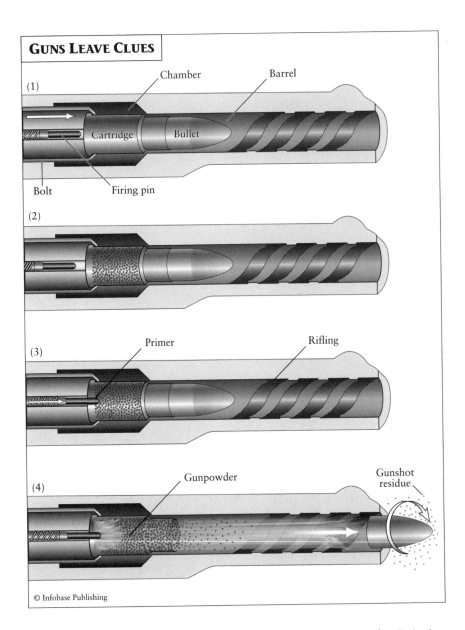

GUNS LEAVE CLUES

(1) Chamber, Barrel, Cartridge, Bullet, Bolt, Firing pin

(2)

(3) Primer, Rifling

(4) Gunpowder, Gunshot residue

© Infobase Publishing

mid-1930s, most large cities in the United States, Canada, Britain, and Europe had set up forensic ballistics laboratories or added this branch of forensic science to existing laboratories. Scientists at

(Opposite page) *The sequence of events that takes place when a gun is fired leaves useful clues for the forensic ballistics scientist. 1. The bolt moves forward, compressing the spring in the firing pin and pushing a cartridge into the chamber of the gun. The cartridge casing receives identifiable scratches in the process. 2. The tension of the spring holds the firing pin back. 3. Pulling the trigger releases the spring and sends the firing pin forward. The pin crushes the primer in the cartridge base and sets it on fire. The pin also leaves a mark on the cartridge base. 4. The primer, in turn, ignites gunpowder in the cartridge. Gas pressure from the gunpowder's miniature explosion pushes the bullet forward and out of the barrel at high speed. As the bullet flies through the gun's rifled barrel, the spiral rifling makes the bullet start spinning. The rifling also leaves a pattern of scratches on the bullet. Gunshot residue, made up of chemicals from the gunpowder, sprays out of the barrel along with the bullet and may mark the hands or clothing of the shooter.*

some of these facilities developed new devices and tests in forensic ballistics during the 1930s, including the periphery camera, which could photograph the whole curved surface of a bullet at once, and a test that could identify gunshot residue on skin. Gunshot residue is made up of chemicals that spray out from a gun when the weapon is fired.

Unfortunately for Goddard, his Chicago laboratory generated more admiration than money. Funding for most enterprises was scarce during the economic depression of the 1930s, and forensic science laboratories were no exception. After working without pay during most of 1934, Goddard resigned as head of the Scientific Crime Detection Laboratory. The city of Chicago bought the laboratory from Northwestern University in 1938 and transferred its equipment to the city police department.

Goddard worked for private firms during the rest of the 1930s and wrote numerous magazine articles on forensic ballistics, crime detection, and military history. He wrote *History of Firearms Identification* in 1936, a book that Colin and Damon Wilson say "is still the classic work on the subject."

When the United States entered World War II in 1941, Goddard rejoined the army. He became the ordnance department's chief historian in 1942. In 1947, after the war ended, Goddard went to Tokyo, Japan, to become assistant chief of the historical branch of the general headquarters of the Far East Command, the United States military government that controlled Japan at the time. Goddard established the Far East Criminal Investigation Laboratory in Tokyo in 1948 and headed it for three years. Military and civilian police all over Asia called on this laboratory for help in solving crimes. Goddard was raised to the rank of full colonel in 1950 and became chief of the historical unit of the Army Medical Service in 1951. He retired in 1954 because of ill health and died on February 22, 1955, in Washington, D.C.

Forensic Ballistics Today

Modern firearms identification experts still use descendants of the comparison microscope and the helixometer to determine whether a particular gun fired a particular bullet. Today's comparison microscopes sometimes include closed-circuit television units and digital cameras.

Forensic ballistics scientists can now consult huge computerized databases, the descendants of Charles Waite's gun catalog. One such database is the General Rifling Characteristic (GRC) file, established by the FBI in 1980. The GRC file contains detailed measurements of the rifling in more than 18,000 types of guns, including the number and size of lands and grooves and the direction in which the spiral twists.

Drugfire, another FBI electronic database (set up in 1989), includes hundreds of thousands of digital images of fired bullets and cartridge casings. Police can compare bullets and casings from crime scenes against these images. Forensic Technology in Montreal, Canada, created a similar system, the Integrated Ballistics Identification System (IBIS), in 1992. In 1999, the FBI and the Bureau of Alcohol, Tobacco and Firearms (ATF) began developing the National Integrated Ballistics Information Network (NIBIN), a program that lets the Drugfire and IBIS databases exchange information.

Forensic ballistic analysts do much more than match bullets to guns. For instance, they study the shape of the holes that bullets make in human flesh or other materials. By comparing these holes with others made by test-firing suspect guns into cardboard, they can determine the flight path of bullets both before and after the bullets struck their target. Computer simulations often aid this process. The shape of bullet holes and the presence or absence of gunshot residue around the holes provide information about how close the shooter was standing to the victim or target. Gunshot residue and burning around a bullet wound show that the gun was near the body when it was fired. Gunshot residue on a person's hands or clothing suggests, but does not prove, that the person recently fired a gun. The person could have picked up the residue by standing nearby when a gun was fired or by handling the gun soon after the firing.

Forensic ballistics, like most other branches of forensic science, is not always accurate. Impacts often distort bullets in ways that make the bullets hard to match to undistorted ones from test firings, for example. Knowing the characteristics of a bullet is useless if detectives cannot find a weapon against whose test firings the bullet can be compared. In spite of these problems, forensic ballistics has helped police departments solve many crimes.

Chronology

A.D. **1000**	Chinese invent gunpowder
1200	Handguns invented in Middle East
1490s	Gunsmiths begin carving spiral grooves (rifling) on the inside of gun barrels
1891	Calvin Hooker Goddard born in Baltimore, Maryland, on October 30
1915	Goddard earns M.D. from Johns Hopkins University medical school
	Farmworker Charles Stielow is convicted of murdering Charles Phelps and Margaret Walcott
1916–20	Goddard serves in U.S. Army Medical Corps
1917	Charles Waite and others review Stielow's conviction and conclude that the murder bullets could not have come from Stielow's gun; Stielow is pardoned

1918–22	Waite assembles catalog of rifling of all models of guns manufactured in the United States and Europe
1920	Two payroll guards are murdered during a robbery on April 15; Italian-born anarchists Nicola Sacco and Bartolomeo Vanzetti are charged with the crime
1920–25	Goddard teaches at several universities, works in private practice as heart specialist, and joins the army ordnance (gunnery) reserve
1921	On July 14, Sacco and Vanzetti are convicted of the murder of the guards and sentenced to death
1923	Waite establishes Bureau of Forensic Ballistics; John H. Fisher invents helixometer; Philip O. Gravelle invents comparison microscope
1925	Goddard joins Bureau of Forensic Ballistics
1926	Waite dies of heart attack on November 14; Goddard becomes head of Bureau of Forensic Ballistics
1927	In June, Goddard is asked to review firearms evidence in Sacco-Vanzetti case; he concludes that the bullets that killed the guards came from Sacco's revolver
	Sacco and Vanzetti are executed on August 23
1929	On February 14, seven gangsters are murdered with machine guns in Chicago, a crime that becomes known as the St. Valentine's Day Massacre; at the request of Chicago police, Goddard examines all police machine guns and concludes that none took part in the shooting
	Two members of grand jury investigating St. Valentine's Day Massacre offer to fund new crime laboratory in Chicago if Goddard will head it; Goddard accepts
	In December, police raid home of professional killer Fred Burke and find weapons, including two Thompson machine guns
1929–30	Goddard visits forensic science laboratories in Europe

1930	Goddard concludes that machine guns found at Burke's home were used in St. Valentine's Day Massacre; Burke is sentenced to life in prison
	Goddard establishes Scientific Crime Detection Laboratory at Northwestern University; he becomes professor of police science at the university
1932	Federal Bureau of Investigation establishes forensic science laboratory, using Goddard's Chicago laboratory as a model
1930s	Most large cities in the United States, Canada, Britain, and Europe establish forensic ballistic laboratories or add this branch of science to existing laboratories by the middle of the decade
	New forensic ballistics devices and tests developed
1934	Goddard resigns from Scientific Crime Detection Laboratory
1936	Goddard writes *History of Firearms Identification*
1938	City of Chicago buys Scientific Crime Detection Laboratory from Northwestern University and reinstalls it as part of police department
1941	Goddard reenlists in U.S. army
1942	Goddard becomes ordnance department's chief historian
1947	Goddard becomes assistant chief of historical branch of general headquarters of Far East Command in Tokyo
1948	Goddard establishes Far East Criminal Investigation Laboratory in Tokyo
1950	Goddard promoted to full colonel
1951	Goddard becomes chief of historical unit of Army Medical Service
1954	Goddard retires
1955	Goddard dies in Washington, D.C., on February 22

1961	Reexamination of ballistic evidence in Sacco-Vanzetti case confirms Goddard's conclusion that the murder bullets came from Sacco's revolver
1980	FBI establishes General Rifling Characteristic database
1983	Second reexamination of ballistic evidence in Sacco-Vanzetti case confirms Goddard's conclusion that the murder bullets came from Sacco's revolver
1989	FBI establishes Drugfire database of bullets and cartridge casings
1992	Forensic Technology in Montreal, Canada, creates Integrated Ballistics Identification System (IBIS)
1999	FBI and Bureau of Alcohol, Tobacco, and Firearms create computer program that allows Drugfire and IBIS systems to exchange data

Further Reading

Books

Wilson, Colin, and Damon Wilson. *Written in Blood: A History of Forensic Detection.* New York: Carroll & Graf reissue, 2003.
> Contains a chapter on forensic ballistics, including the work of Charles Waite, Calvin Goddard, and Herbert McDonell.

Yeatts, Tabatha. *Forensics: Solving the Crime.* Minneapolis: Oliver Press, 2001.
> For young adults. Contains a chapter on Waite, Goddard, and the development of forensic ballistics.

Articles

Bodayla, Stephen D. "Calvin Hooker Goddard." In *Dictionary of American Biography, Supplement 5: 1951–1955.* New York: American Council of Learned Societies, 1977.
> Biographical article summarizing Goddard's career in forensic ballistics.

Goddard, Calvin. "Forensic Ballistics." *Army Ordnance Magazine,* November–December 1925.

Technical article describing the work of Charles Waite's Bureau of Forensic Ballistics in New York City, including use of new inventions such as the comparison microscope.

Hamby, James E. "The History of Firearm and Toolmark Identification." *Association of Firearm and Toolmark Examiners Journal* 31 (Summer 1999).

Extensive history of forensic ballistics, covering the period from 1835 to 1999.

Ramsland, Katherine. "Ballistics: The Science of Guns." Available online. URL: http://www.crimelibrary.com/criminal_mind/forensics/ballistics/1.html. Accessed on September 22, 2005.

Series of five articles on forensic ballistics, part of the Court TV Crime Library, that includes discussions of the Sacco-Vanzetti case and the St. Valentine's Day Massacre, as well as the history of the field and description of modern forensic ballistics.

LIAR, LIAR

LEONARDE KEELER AND THE POLYGRAPH

From ancient times, crime investigators have looked for ways to tell whether the suspects and witnesses they interviewed were lying or speaking the truth. In China around 1000 B.C., for example, a person being questioned had to take a mouthful of dry rice, then spit it out. If the rice was wet when spit out, the person was believed to be telling the truth; if it was dry, the person was lying. This test was based on the idea that if a person was lying, nervousness would make his or her mouth dry.

The Chinese test grew out of an important observation: Strong emotions cause physical changes in the body. Several inventors in the early 20th century, especially police scientist Leonarde Keeler, drew on that same observation to design a machine that they claimed could determine scientifically whether a person is lying or not. Their creation, the polygraph (informally called the lie detector), is still widely used, but critics have raised serious questions about its accuracy.

The First Lie Detectors

The search for a dependable way to identify liars began, like so many other parts of forensic science, in the late 19th century. In 1885, Italian criminologist and statistician Cesare Lombroso recorded suspects' blood pressure as police questioned them. Lombroso knew that stress—tension caused by unpleasant conditions or events—produces a rise in blood pressure, and he believed that someone who was lying would feel more stress during questioning than a person who was telling the truth.

Following in Lombroso's footsteps, U.S. scientist William Moulton Marston invented a device that measured blood pressure automatically during questioning. Marston was a Harvard University graduate student in psychology in 1913, when he created his machine. He tested it on German prisoners of war during World War I.

Leonarde Keeler invented the modern polygraph, or lie detector, in the late 1920s. Scientists disagree about the accuracy of this machine, but criminals' belief in its power often makes them confess. (Corbis)

In the same year that Marston announced his invention, Vittorio Benussi, an Italian psychologist, recommended a different test for lying. Benussi's test focused on breathing, or respiration. Breathing speeds up during stress, and Benussi, like Lombroso, assumed that liars would be under more stress than people who told the truth.

John Larson, a medical student at the University of California, Berkeley, as well as a sergeant in the Berkeley police force, combined Marston's and Benussi's ideas. In 1921, Larson invented a machine that measured blood pressure, pulse (heartbeat), and respiration continuously during an interview and recorded them as rising or falling pen lines on graph paper. He called his creation a polygraph, from Greek words meaning "many writings," because the device produced several tracings at the same time. Larson and Berkeley's police chief, August Vollmer, tested the device on 4,000 criminal suspects in the early 1920s. They found that simply connecting people to the machine often was enough to frighten them into confessing.

CONNECTIONS: WONDER WOMAN AND HER MAGIC LASSO

William Marston's lie detector was never widely used, but he gained fame in the 1940s for a very different achievement: He created Wonder Woman, the first female comic-book superhero.

In 1940, well established in his career as a psychologist, Marston became a consultant for a business that published many superhero stories. (The company later became DC Comics.) Comic-book characters with special powers, such as Superman and Batman, had first appeared in the late 1930s and were becoming very popular. Most fans of superhero comics were boys and young men, but Marston believed that such stories should also reflect female values. He once wrote:

> Wonder Woman is psychological propaganda for the new type of woman who should, I believe, rule the world. There isn't love enough in the male organism to run this planet peacefully. . . . What woman lacks is the dominance or self-assertive power to put over and enforce her . . . desires. I have given Wonder Woman this dominant force but have kept her loving, tender, maternal [motherly] and feminine in every other way.

Wonder Woman made her first appearance in the December 1941 issue of *All Star Comics,* with a story written by Marston (under the pen name of Charles Moulton) and drawn by Harry Peter. In that story, Steve Trevor, an American pilot, crash-lands his plane on Paradise Island, the home of a clan of women warriors—the Amazons described in ancient Greek legends. Diana, the Amazon princess, falls in love with Trevor and follows him back to "Man's World," where she becomes a crime-fighting superheroine. Fittingly for the inventor of the first lie detector, Marston gave Diana, or Wonder Woman, a magic lasso that forced anyone it encircled to tell the truth.

The *Frye* Decision

August Vollmer and a few others hailed the polygraph as a useful new tool, but the courts were less welcoming. In a case involving lie detector evidence—from William Marston's machine, not Larson's—the District of Columbia Court of Appeals produced a historic decision on December 3, 1923. This decision not only affected the future of polygraphs but also determined what scientific evidence could be used in a courtroom for most of the 20th century.

The case was called *Frye v. United States*. James T. Frye, who had been convicted of murder, appealed his conviction because, he said, the court had wrongly prevented his attorneys from introducing testimony from Marston about the "systolic blood pressure deception test," which Frye had passed. In the court's decision, Chief Justice Smyth wrote, "While courts will go a long way in admitting expert testimony deduced from a well-organized scientific principle or discovery, the thing from which the [expert witness's] deduction is made must be sufficiently established to have gained general acceptance in the particular field to which it belongs." Smyth concluded that the "systolic blood pressure deception test has not yet gained such . . . scientific recognition" because it was still a very new invention. Therefore, although police could use lie detectors when questioning suspects, the results of the tests could not be admitted as evidence in court.

Keeler Improves the Polygraph

John Larson, who saw the polygraph primarily as a tool for medicine rather than law enforcement, stopped using the machine in crime detection after a few years. Another Berkeley police officer, Leonarde Keeler, then took over the device and began improving it.

Keeler, a Berkeley native, had been born on October 30, 1903. His parents named him after the Renaissance genius Leonardo da Vinci (1452–1519). When Keeler was in high school, his father introduced him to August Vollmer, a family friend. Keeler immediately became interested in crime detection and, especially, in the "lie box" that John Larson was developing. He watched Larson interview a burglary suspect with the device and went with Larson to test the machine on patients in state mental hospitals.

Vollmer left Berkeley in 1923 to become chief of police in Los Angeles, and Keeler went with him. Keeler enrolled in the University of California, Los Angeles, and paid for his education with a variety of jobs, including "milking" venom from rattlesnakes that he and a friend captured in the Los Angeles hills. They sold the venom to a laboratory that used it in a treatment for snakebite.

Vollmer and Keeler returned to the San Francisco Bay area later in the 1920s, and Keeler continued his studies at Stanford University in Palo Alto, where he majored in psychology. While working toward his degree, Keeler also improved the polygraph, which he patented in 1925. Around 1926, besides making the machine smaller and more dependable, he added a third measurement to the two that Larson's device had provided. This measurement, the galvanic skin response (GSR), shows the degree to which a person's skin conducts electricity. This conductivity, in turn, depends on the amount of sweat that the skin is producing. An increase in sweat is another sign of stress.

Popularizing the Lie Detector

Leonarde Keeler joined John Larson at the Institute for Juvenile Research in Chicago in 1929. The two men and their coworkers tested the improved polygraph on convicts in Joliet State Prison and on inmates of mental institutions. When Calvin Goddard established the Scientific Crime Detection Laboratory at Northwestern University Law School, near Chicago, in 1930, Keeler became part of the laboratory's staff.

Keeler remained with the crime detection laboratory until 1933. He then worked as a private consultant in Chicago, conducting polygraph tests at the request of police departments and businesses. He also publicized the polygraph and persuaded many police departments to adopt it. He maintained that, when used by experienced operators, the polygraph accurately distinguished between truth and falsehood 90 percent of the time. With others, Keeler designed several forms of questioning used in polygraph tests, including the most common type employed today. He and Fred Inbau established the first school that trained people to use the polygraph and analyze its tracings.

Keeler helped the U.S. Army teach officers to use the polygraph during World War II. In the late 1940s, he taught government agencies and businesses how to screen employees with the machine and uncover spies or other criminals. He also took part in many criminal investigations, one of which was made into a movie, *Call Northside 777* (1948). Keeler played himself in the film, which showed how a polygraph test helped to free a man who had spent 11 years in prison for a murder he had not committed. Keeler died of a stroke during a vacation at Sturgeon Bay, Wisconsin, on September 20, 1949.

The Polygraph Test

A polygraph test begins with a long interview that takes place before the machine is brought out. During this interview, the tester asks the person to be tested about his or her background and health. The

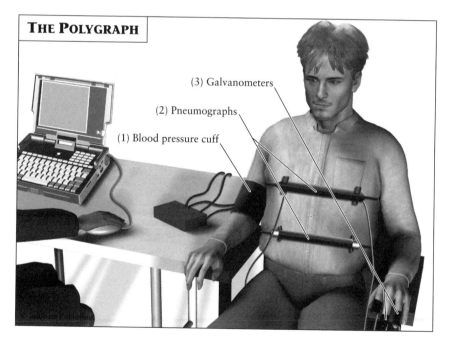

THE POLYGRAPH

(3) Galvanometers

(2) Pneumographs

(1) Blood pressure cuff

Sensors attached to a polygraph detect changes in several kinds of body functions that are thought to reflect the stress of lying. 1. A cuff around the arm measures blood pressure and heartbeat rate. 2. Sensors around the chest measure breathing. 3. Sensors attached to the fingers measure the skin's response to electricity (galvanic skin response), which reflects the amount of sweat that the skin is producing.

tester also explains how the device works and reviews the questions that will be asked during the test. (The American Polygraph Association emphasizes that "there are no surprise or trick questions" in a polygraph examination.) If the test is part of a criminal investigation, the person being examined will be advised of his or her rights and may have an attorney present during testing. No one can be forced to take a polygraph test.

The examination itself usually lasts about two hours. At the start of the test, the interviewer places rubber tubes around the person's chest and abdomen. The tubes stretch and contract as the person breathes, and the machine measures these changes. An inflatable cuff around the arm, much like the one used in doctors' offices, measures blood pressure and heartbeat rate. Metal plates attached to the fingers measure the galvanic skin response. Styluses connected to these devices trace continuous lines on a moving roll of paper during the test. The points at which questions are asked are also marked on the paper, so an analyst can tell which part of the tracings was made during the response to each question.

Once the person being tested is connected to the polygraph machine, the interviewer asks him or her approximately 10 questions. Half of these, called control questions, have nothing to do with the crime or other issue being investigated. Measurements made when the person answers these questions give the tester a baseline of responses for that person. The rest of the questions relate to information that the police or other agencies want to know. The complete set of questions is repeated three times, with rest periods in between.

After the testing session is over, the tester analyzes the tracings, often with the help of a computer. He or she then decides whether the person was truthful, dishonest, or cannot be classified. If the analyst cannot tell whether the person was telling the truth or lying, the test may be repeated on a different day. If the analyst concludes that the person was lying, investigators try to discover the truth in further interviews.

In 1981, University of Minnesota psychologist David Lykken, a critic of standard polygraph tests, created a different type of test interview that he claims is more useful in investigating crimes than the control-question method. Questions in Lykken's interviews focus on "guilty knowledge"—facts that only the person who committed the crime or someone who has heard about the criminal's activities will know. Even if the person being tested does not admit to this knowledge, Lykken and his supporters say, the person will show an emotional reaction to questions about it that an innocent individual will not. That reaction will be reflected in the polygraph tracings.

True or False?

The polygraph has been controversial from its beginning. For example, J. Edgar Hoover, director of the FBI from 1924 to 1972, told his agents not to use the machine because he thought it unreliable. On the other hand, William J. Warner, a special agent in the FBI's polygraph unit, stated in 2005 that "polygraph testing offers investigators a . . . tool they can employ in interviews to help them obtain . . . valuable information."

The main problem with the polygraph, critics say, is that no one has ever proved that lying dependably produces the kinds of changes that the machine measures. These changes are connected with nervousness, stress, or strong emotion, but an innocent person accused of a crime is as likely to have such feelings as a guilty one. In an evaluation of polygraph testing published in 2003, a committee of the National Research Council, part of the U.S. National Academy of Sciences, wrote, "Almost a century of research in scientific psychology and physiology provides little basis for the expectation that a polygraph test could have extremely high accuracy." Furthermore, people can learn to control the reactions that a polygraph measures. A 1994 study showed that when people trained to "beat the machine" were tested, half of them were able to fool the polygraph analysts.

Polygraph interviewers and analysts also make mistakes, especially if they are inexperienced or poorly trained. As of 2005, only 29 states required polygraph analysts to be licensed or certified. To obtain a license, an analyst usually must take a six-week program of courses at a polygraph school, complete an internship or training period during which experienced analysts review the trainee's conclusions, and undergo a final examination.

Even the American Polygraph Association, which claims that the polygraph is accurate 92 to 98 percent of the time when properly used, says that "a valid examination requires a combination of a properly trained examiner, a polygraph instrument that records as a minimum cardiovascular [blood pressure and pulse rate], respiratory, and electrodermal [galvanic skin response] activity, and the proper administration of an accepted testing procedure and scoring system." In a 1981 study, the most experienced of six polygraph interpreters made mistakes 18 percent of the time, and the least experienced was in error 55 percent of the time.

Defenders of polygraphs say that the machines are no more inaccurate than most other technologies in forensic science. For example, Katherine Ramsland writes in an article in Court TV's online crime library, "The polygraph appears to compare favorably with evidence like fiber analysis, ballistics comparison, and blood analysis." Polygraph supporters such as the FBI's William Warner also maintain that the machines can be useful to police and government agents even if test results are not very accurate, simply because many people *think* the devices cannot be fooled. Fear of being exposed by the "lie detector," Warner says, has often made suspects confess to crimes or give investigators information that might not otherwise have been revealed. "I don't know anything about lie detectors," former president Richard Nixon stated in 1971, "other than that they scare the hell out of people." Warner thinks that may be enough.

Polygraph Evidence in Court

In spite of questions about the polygraph's accuracy, police in many states regularly give lie detector tests to suspects in major crimes. They may also give the tests to witnesses if the witnesses' testimony seems doubtful. The National Research Council committee supported forensic use of polygraphs, stating that when asking about specific incidents such as crimes, "polygraph tests can discriminate lying from truth telling at rates well above chance, though well below perfection."

I Was There: The "Unbeatable" Machine

In a 1931 article in the *Proceedings of the International Association of Chiefs of Police,* Leonarde Keeler described a case in which he used a polygraph to extract a confession. A burglar opening a safe in an apartment had been interrupted when the apartment's owner came home. The burglar tried to leave by a window but became entangled in a heavy curtain. Frustrated, the criminal turned around, shot the owner, and ran out the door.

The police brought in four suspects for polygraph testing. Keeler described the procedure:

> We put them on the machine one at a time, and at first ran along normal about four minutes, to ascertain their . . . fluctuations [variations] which are normal to that individual. Then we asked three or four questions that had nothing to do with the crime. . . . Then we ask[ed] questions such as: "Do you own an apartment on Main Street?" That was the name of the street that this burglarized apartment was on. . . . "Have you some heavy plush curtains on your windows? Have you a safe in your apartment?"

These men proved to be innocent of the crime and, Keeler said, "thought we were crazy asking them such foolish questions." However, Keeler reported:

> The next day a [fifth] burglar was brought in. We gave him the test, and he responded violently, gave great fluctuations in blood pressure [and] respiration whenever we mentioned any description . . . of that apartment house. On the third test we turned him around so he could watch the machine, and suggested that he watch the needles carefully, and told him what they would do whenever he lied. In the middle of the test he confessed and said that he saw he couldn't beat it, and he told us the complete story [of the robbery], which was later verified.

Many judges still do not allow evidence from polygraph tests to be presented during trials. Judges have more freedom to decide to use polygraph evidence than they did in the 1920s, however, because of a 1993 Supreme Court decision in the case of *Daubert v. Merrell Dow Pharmaceuticals.* That case did not involve lie detectors, but the decision applies to all types of scientific evidence and expert tes-

---

ISSUES: SCREENING FOR SPIES

In the 1940s and 1950s, many employers gave polygraph tests to their workers or to people applying for jobs in the hope of screening out those who might steal at work, reveal secret information, or commit other crimes. More than 80 percent of all polygraph tests were used for this purpose at one time.

Several groups objected to this kind of testing. First, critics say, screening tests are far more likely to be inaccurate than tests related to specific events because the testers must necessarily ask more general questions, such as "Have you ever stolen anything?" or "Have you ever revealed secret information to an unauthorized person?" People may genuinely disagree about which answers to such questions are truthful. The connection between past actions and future ones is also open to debate. Does the fact that someone once used illegal drugs mean that the person is likely to become a spy?

Opponents of employee screening also claim that making people take lie detector tests in order to obtain or keep jobs invades their privacy and violates their civil rights. A test mistakenly interpreted as showing that someone was lying could ruin a career, they point out. Even honest employees may be so afraid of such a result that they will not apply for jobs that require the tests. Companies and the government therefore will be deprived of potentially valuable workers.

In answer to these complaints, Congress passed the Employee Polygraph Protection Act in 1988. This act bars private businesses from using polygraph tests for employee screening under most circumstances. The law does not apply to law enforcement, military, or government agencies, however. Agencies that deal with nuclear weapons or other restricted subjects, such as the Department of Energy (DOE), the FBI, and the Central Intelligence Agency (CIA), still use polygraph tests in attempts to identify spies or terrorists.

timony in trials, polygraph tests included. Essentially, the Supreme Court ruled that individual judges should decide what scientific testimony to allow in their courtrooms—a less strict standard than the *Frye* requirement of general scientific acceptance. Judges are most likely to admit a polygraph test as evidence when attorneys for both plaintiff and defendant agree in advance (before the test is given) to accept it.

The National Research Council committee was highly critical of using polygraph tests for screening employees. "Available evidence indicates that polygraph testing as currently used has extremely serious limitations in such screening applications," the committee wrote. In fact, the group stated, too much reliance on polygraph tests to protect national security could actually undermine security by wasting resources and producing a false sense that possible spying or sabotage is being kept under control, thus leading agencies to relax other security measures. The American Polygraph Association replied that the report "does not adequately recognize the many successes of [the] polygraph in both the criminal specific arena and in National Security." The association insists that polygraph tests used for screening are almost as reliable as those given to detect specific crimes.

Other Ways to Spot Lying

Several inventors have proposed tests that might replace polygraph examinations as ways of finding out whether someone is lying. One alternative test produces a graph reflecting the sounds of a person's voice as the person answers questions. Analysts look for rises in pitch and other voice changes thought to be associated with lying. The voice stress test, however, has found even less scientific support than the polygraph test.

A second alternative uses a technique called functional magnetic resonance imaging (fMRI) to measure changes in blood flow in the brain. Many scientists who study the brain use fMRI, but whether it will prove to be a good way to detect liars remains to be seen.

Iowa neuroscientist Lawrence A. Farwell has invented a third test that he calls "brain fingerprinting." Farwell's test employs electroencephalography (EEG), a widely accepted technique that measures electrical impulses from the brain using sensors in a headband. Brain fingerprinting works something like the guilty knowledge form of polygraph testing, except that the testing is conducted through words or pictures on a computer screen rather than through spoken questions. Some of the words or pictures are connected with the crime about which the suspect or witness is being questioned, while others are not. In theory, when the person being tested sees items that are familiar to him or her, the person's brain will produce a particular pattern of discharges that an analyst can recognize. Critics point out that, even if the theory proves to be correct, the test probably could not distinguish between familiarity produced by committing a crime and familiarity produced simply by having seen or even read about the crime. Brain fingerprinting, like all other alternatives to the polygraph proposed so far, is still considered experimental at best.

Chronology

1000 B.C.	Chinese test people for lying by having them take a mouthful of rice and spit it out; if the rice is dry, the person is considered nervous and therefore most likely guilty
1885	Cesare Lombroso measures blood pressure of suspects during police interviews to determine whether they are lying
1903	Leonarde Keeler born in Berkeley, California, on October 30
1913	William Moulton Marston invents machine that measures blood pressure automatically during questioning
	Vittorio Benussi recommends measuring breathing as a way of identifying liars
1921	John Larson invents the polygraph
1923	In *Frye v. United States,* District of Columbia appeals court rules that polygraph testing is not respected enough by the scientific community to be allowed as evidence in court

	Keeler accompanies police chief August Vollmer to Los Angeles and enrolls at the University of California, Los Angeles
1925	Keeler patents his version of the polygraph
1926	Keeler improves the polygraph by adding measurement of galvanic skin response, determined by sweating
1929	Keeler joins Larson at Institute for Juvenile Research in Chicago
1930–33	Keeler works at Calvin Goddard's Scientific Crime Detection Laboratory
1930s	Keeler works as private consultant; persuades police departments to adopt polygraph; designs basic form of questioning in polygraph test; sets up school to train people to use polygraph
1940s	Keeler trains people in military and government agencies to use polygraph to screen employees; he takes part in criminal investigations
1949	Keeler dies of a stroke at Sturgeon Bay, Wisconsin, on September 20
1950s	Many employers give polygraph tests to workers and people applying for jobs
1981	David Lykken develops "guilty knowledge" form of questioning for polygraph tests
1988	Congress passes Employee Polygraph Protection Act, barring private employers from giving polygraph tests to employees or people applying for jobs
1993	U.S. Supreme Court decision in *Daubert v. Merrell Dow Pharmaceuticals* allows judges to decide which forms of scientific evidence to permit in court
2003	Committee of the National Research Council publishes report criticizing reliability of polygraph testing, particularly in employment screening

Further Reading

Books

Board on Behavioral, Cognitive, and Sensory Sciences and Education, Committee on National Statistics. *The Polygraph and Lie Detection.* Washington, D.C.: National Academies Press, 2003.
> This report by a committee of the National Research Council, part of the U.S. National Academy of Sciences, concludes that the polygraph is too inaccurate to be valuable, especially when used to screen government employees as a way of protecting national security. A summary of the report is available online at http://www.nap.edu/books/0309084369/html/1.html.

Evans, Colin. *Murder 2: The Second Casebook of Forensic Detection.* Hoboken, N.J.: Wiley, 2004.
> Contains short chapters on the polygraph (lie detector) and on brain fingerprinting.

Wilson, Colin, and Damon Wilson. *Written in Blood: A History of Forensic Detection.* New York: Carroll & Graf reissue, 2003.
> Contains material on the development and early uses of the polygraph.

Articles

Faigman, David L., Stephen E. Feinberg, and Paul C. Stern. "The Limits of the Polygraph." *Issues in Science and Technology* 20 (Fall 2003): 40–46.
> The authors, who took part in the National Research Council review of the polygraph, strongly criticize the use of polygraph tests for forensic purposes.

Keeler, Leonarde. "Lie Detector Applications." *Proceedings of the IACP [International Association of Chiefs of Police],* 1931, p. 184. (Reprinted in *Polygraph* 23 (1994): 149–151.)
> Keeler describes several cases in which he used the polygraph to solve crimes and persuade suspects to confess.

———. "A Method for Detecting Deception." *American Journal of Police Science* 1 (1930): 38–52. (Reprinted in *Polygraph* 23 (1994): 134–144.)
> Keeler's description of the history of the polygraph and the way his machine works. This issue of *Polygraph* also contains a number of other articles by Keeler.

"Making Windows in Men's Souls: Lie Detection." *Economist* 372 (July 10, 2004): 72.

> Describes several alternatives to polygraph testing.

Ramsland, Katherine. "The Polygraph." Available online. URL: htttp://www.crimelibrary.com/criminal_mind/forensics/polygraph/1.html. Accessed on September 22, 2005.

> This series of articles, part of the Court TV Crime Library, cites cases in which the polygraph has been used, describes the two most common purposes for its use, and discusses criticisms of the technology.

Ruscio, John. "Exploring Controversies in the Art and Science of Polygraph Testing." *Skeptical Inquirer* 29 (January–February 2005): 34–39.

> Criticizes the accuracy of polygraph testing. Claims that the "guilty knowledge" version of questioning is more accurate than the common control-question test.

Stevens, Viola. "Biography of Leonarde Keeler." *Polygraph* 23 (1994): 118–126.

> Provides biographical information on Keeler and his development of the polygraph.

Warner, William J. "Polygraph Testing: A Utilitarian Tool." *FBI Law Enforcement Bulletin* 74 (April 2005): 10–13.

> Concludes that, even if polygraphs are not especially accurate, they are useful in investigating crimes because belief in their power frightens people into confessing crimes or providing information that investigators might not otherwise obtain.

Web Site

American Polygraph Association (APA). URL: http://www.polygraph.org. Accessed on September 22, 2005.

> The APA claims to be the leading association of polygraph professionals. It seeks to establish standards of training, techniques, and ethics for polygraph examiners and to present a positive view of polygraphs to law enforcement agencies and the public. Its site includes answers to frequently asked questions about polygraphs, accounts of research on the validity of polygraphs, and a reply to the critical National Research Council report issued in 2003.

7
VOICEPRINTS

LAWRENCE KERSTA AND VOICE IDENTIFICATION

Sometimes the only clue to a criminal's identity that police and forensic scientists have is a voice: a telephoned bomb threat, perhaps, or a demand for a ransom payment to save a kidnapped person's life. If the voice has been recorded, that one clue may be enough—thanks to Lawrence G. Kersta, a physicist and engineer at Bell Telephone Laboratories in Murray Hill, New Jersey. Kersta invented the sound spectrograph, a machine that turns recorded sounds into visual graphs. Analysts can use these graphs, called spectrograms or voiceprints, to compare two recordings of speech and determine whether they were made by the same person.

Visual Speech

The first person to try to make sound visible was Melville Bell, the father of telephone inventor Alexander Graham Bell. In 1867, Melville Bell, an expert on philology (the study of language) and phonetics (the study of spoken sounds), created a system of handwritten symbols that could represent any spoken sound on paper. He called his system "visual speech." Bell's notation accurately pictured the tiny variations in the way different people pronounce the same words. Alexander Graham Bell later used his father's system in his own efforts to teach deaf people to speak.

Bell Laboratories engineers invented an early form of the sound spectrograph, or automatic sound wave analyzer, in 1941. Military

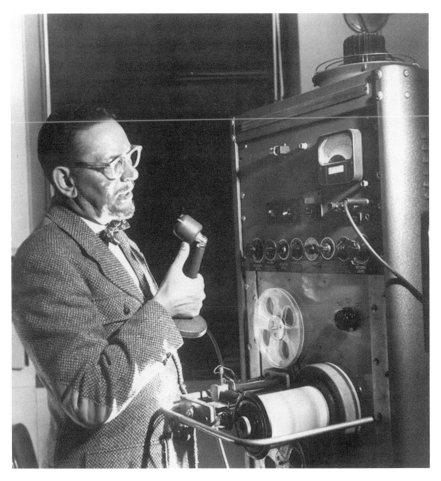

Bell Telephone Laboratories engineer Lawrence G. Kersta invented the sound spectrograph, a machine that turns spoken words or other sounds into visible tracings. Some forensic analysts use the sound spectrograph to identify individual voices. (Lucent Technologies Inc.)

intelligence officers during World War II hoped to use the device to identify voices making German military communications over the radio. Tracking such voices might help them discover enemy spies or give them clues about the movements of German troops. The machine was not very effective, however, and the war ended before it could be improved.

(Opposite page) *In the classic sound spectrograph, sounds are recorded on a magnetic disk and sent to an amplifier, which makes the sound more intense. The sounds then go through a scanner or frequency analyzer, which separates the sounds into different frequencies. (Frequency is a measurement of how often the molecules of the air vibrate as sound waves pass them.) A filter selects a group of frequencies and, with the help of the analyzer, converts them into electrical signals. These signals move the penlike stylus, which marks paper on the recording drum. The stylus produces a series of jagged lines that show both the frequency and the intensity, or loudness, of the sounds. The process is repeated with other groups of frequencies. Today many parts of a sound spectrograph are computerized.*

Lawrence Kersta was one of the engineers who created the sound spectrograph. Born in New Jersey around 1902, he earned a master's degree in physics from Columbia University in New York. He began working for Bell in the late 1930s.

Sound spectrographs were all but forgotten until about 1960, when police in New York City received a series of telephone calls threatening to place bombs on planes. The police recorded some of the calls, and someone remembered Kersta and his wartime machine. The FBI brought the recordings to Kersta, who by then was a senior engineer in Bell Laboratories' department of acoustic and speech research. They asked him to create an improved spectrograph that might help them identify the speaker on the tapes.

The Sound Spectrograph

Kersta's new sound spectrograph had four parts: a tape recorder-player, a scanner or frequency analyzer, a filter, and a stylus. The tape machine recorded voices and played back tapes made on other machines. The scanner analyzed the sounds of a taped voice electronically and sent the result through the filter. The stylus, a penlike instrument, recorded the output on electrically sensitive paper attached to a turning drum. Modern spectrographs also often include a computer to improve recording quality and make comparison of voices faster and easier.

The spectrograph's printout is called a spectrogram. Each spectrogram shows 2.5 seconds of spoken sounds, represented as a

SOUND SPECTROGRAPH

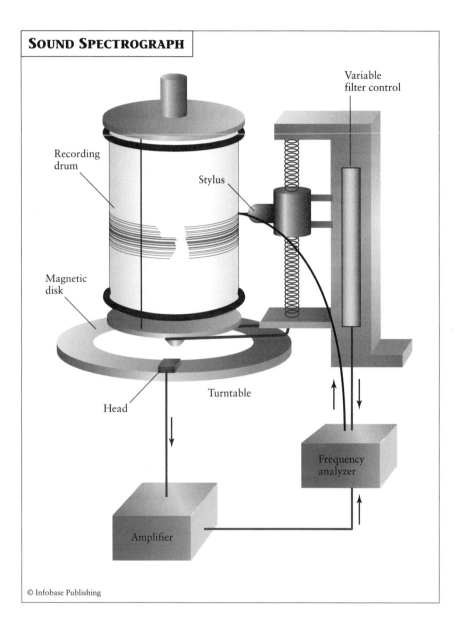

Variable
filter control

Recording
drum

Stylus

Magnetic
disk

Head

Turntable

Frequency
analyzer

Amplifier

© Infobase Publishing

graph. The vertical axis of the graph shows the frequencies of the
sounds—how often the molecules of the air vibrate as the sound
waves pass them. (Humans hear frequencies as pitch. High-fre-

quency tones have a higher pitch than tones with a low frequency.) The filter in the spectrograph breaks the sounds being analyzed into small bands or groups of frequencies, and the spectrogram pictures the energy levels within each group.

The spectrogram reflects the fact that each sound of the human voice actually consists of many sounds occurring at the same time. The most important of these sounds are called fundamentals. Fainter overtones called harmonics occur at pitches above those of the fundamentals. The spectrogram shows the frequencies of both fundamentals and harmonics.

The horizontal axis in a spectrogram shows time. The spectrogram also reveals the volume, or loudness, of each tone, which is a reflection of the amount of energy in each sound wave. The louder a tone is, the darker the line representing it appears on the spectrogram.

Spoken "Fingerprints"

After two years of research involving spectrograms of 50,000 voices, Lawrence Kersta concluded in an article published in *Nature* in 1962 that each person's voice produces unique sound spectrograms. He claimed that sound spectrography could be used to tell one person's voice from another with an accuracy greater than 99 percent. Even when professional mimics were asked to imitate others' voices, Kersta wrote, he could easily separate the original voices from the imitations by looking at their spectrograms.

Kersta believed in the accuracy of spectrograms so strongly that he began calling them "voiceprints" to suggest that they would prove as useful in identification as fingerprints. He trademarked the term and left Bell Laboratories in 1964 to set up his own business, Voiceprint Laboratories Corporation. In 1973, he sold the company, which made and sold sound spectrographs, to Rik Alexanderson, one of his employees. Kersta traveled around the world during the 1960s and 1970s as the guest of governments and police departments, demonstrating the sound spectrograph and showing how it could be used to solve crimes. He died in Miami, Florida, around 1995.

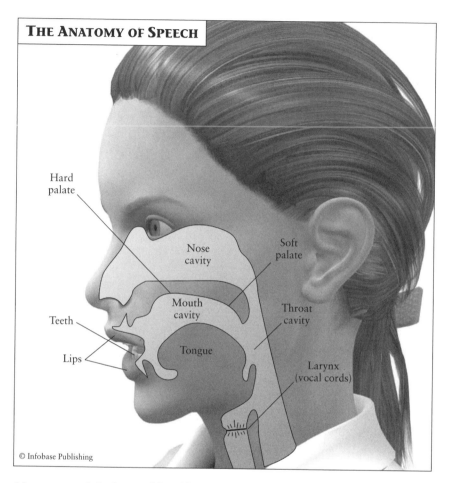

THE ANATOMY OF SPEECH

Hard palate

Nose cavity

Soft palate

Mouth cavity

Throat cavity

Teeth

Tongue

Lips

Larynx (vocal cords)

© Infobase Publishing

Many parts of the face and head help to shape speech. Speech sounds come from the vibration of the vocal cords inside the larynx, or voicebox. The cavities of the mouth, nose, and throat act as resonators, making the sounds louder. The teeth, lips, tongue, and hard and soft palate are the articulators that shape the sounds into speech.

Unique Voices

Lawrence Kersta was sure that each person's voice is like no other because speaking is such a complex task, involving many parts of the mouth and throat. The sounds of speech come from vibrations of the vocal cords inside the larynx, or voice box, in the throat. These vibrations make air molecules move, creating sound waves. The cavities of the mouth, throat, and nose act as resonators, shaping the waves and amplifying them (making the sounds louder). Muscles controlling the lips, teeth, tongue, soft palate, and jaw are the articulators that form the tones from the vocal cords into particular spoken sounds.

CONNECTIONS: COMPUTER VOICE RECOGNITION

Sound spectrograms and analysis of voices have many applications outside of forensic science. Scientists studying language and therapists trying to help people with speech or hearing problems use this technology, for example. Voice identification is sometimes used for security purposes as well.

Computer scientists have developed programs whose purpose is to identify spoken words rather than individual speakers. Some businesses use computers that can recognize a limited range of speech as part of automated services for making movie or airline reservations, for example. Other programs let computers transform spoken dictation into text or allow disabled people to give spoken orders to a computer or other machines.

The first task of a computerized voice-recognition program, whether it is used to identify crime suspects or reserve theater seats, is to transform analog audio information into a digital form that the computer can use. The computer then compares the digital signal to a database of words, syllables, or individual sounds (phonemes) that are likely to occur in that program's application. The program determines what the speaker probably said and responds accordingly.

Translating speech into meaning is tricky, both because people's voices differ and because many words sound alike. For example, the phrases "How to recognize speech using common sense" and "How to wreck a nice beach you sing calm incense" sound almost exactly the same when spoken. A human who understands English will realize immediately that only the first phrase makes sense, but a computer might not be able to guess which of the phrases was spoken. To improve computers' interpretation of spoken words, researchers are developing programs that analyze grammar as well as sound.

The size and shape of each of these parts of the human head varies from person to person, accounting for some of the differences in voices. Other variations come from the way people learn to speak. People in different parts of a country speak with different accents, for example. Some people run their words together, while others talk with pauses between their words. Kersta believed that the combination of the physical differences in the size and shape of speech organs and the learned differences in the way people speak made the chance that two people would have voices similar enough to be confused on voiceprints "remote."

Scientists who have studied sound spectrograms disagree about whether Kersta was right in believing that each person's voice is unique. No one has proved that this is so. Even supporters such as Oscar Tosi of Michigan State University have said that they dislike the term *voiceprint* because it suggests a greater degree of precision than may be justified.

Accurate voice identification is difficult because individual voices change constantly. No one says the same word or speech sound twice with exactly the same frequencies and intensities. Emotion, physical health, and changes such as the wearing of dentures (false teeth) can affect the sound of a person's voice. Voices also alter, sometimes strikingly, with age. If a person moves from one country or region to another, his or her accent may change. However, experienced voice analysts claim that they can recognize these variations within a voice and distinguish them from differences between one person's voice and another's.

Voiceprints in Court

Kersta's voiceprint technology found a warm welcome in Michigan. The Michigan state police set up a voice identification unit in 1966 and hired Kersta to train officers to use his machines and analyze the resulting spectrograms. For a long time, police in other states sent recordings to the Michigan laboratory when they needed expert spectrographic analysis.

Sound spectrograph evidence was first admitted into a court in 1967 during a military trial (court-martial), *United States v.*

Wright. An appeals court upheld the trial judge's decision to accept the evidence, but one of the appeals judges, Judge Ferguson, wrote a lengthy dissent, saying that voice identification by sound spectrograph did not meet the *Frye* standard of general acceptance by the scientific community. In the late 1960s and 1970s, when sound spectrograph technology was fairly new, many other judges refused to allow its use in trials for the same reason. More and more courts permitted voiceprint analysts to testify as time went on, however. Courts in most states today decide on a case-by-case basis whether to admit or deny voiceprint analysis in particular trials. Judges' decisions depend on the quality of recordings and the experience of analysts who will testify, for example. When voiceprint evidence is admitted, it is used mainly to support other evidence.

"Garbage in, Garbage out"

Sound spectrographs are used for many scientific purposes. The accuracy of the machines themselves is rarely questioned. However, the spectrograms they produce can be only as good as the recordings from which the spectrograms are made. As computer scientists say, "Garbage in, garbage out": If data being analyzed are incorrect or unclear, conclusions drawn from the analysis will probably be incorrect as well.

In the case of voice recordings, the "garbage" may come from sounds in the background, such as other voices, music, or the noise of machinery. These forms of interference can make obtaining accurate spectrograms of a voice difficult or impossible. Voice analysts Michael McDermott and Tom Owen say that some examiners reject up to 60 percent of the samples of unknown voices sent to them because the quality of the samples is too poor for accurate analysis. The lower the quality of the recording of an unknown voice, the longer a sample of speech an analyst will need in order to make an identification. A long sample will also be needed if the unknown speaker is trying to disguise his or her voice.

When suspects' voices are recorded for comparison against a crime-related recording, the analyst usually can control the environment and recording quality. The analyst will strive for a clear recording, but he or she may also try to duplicate the conditions

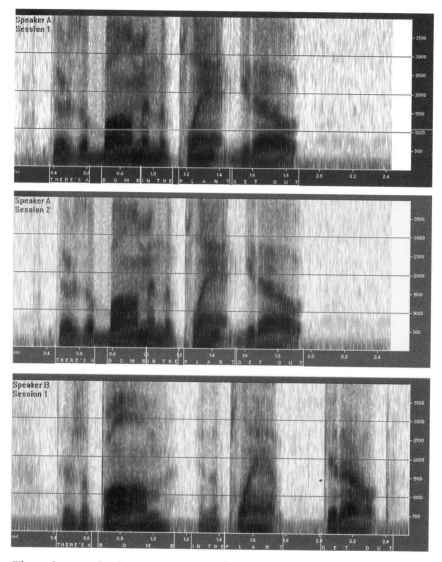

These photographs show spectrograms of spoken sounds, which inventor Lawrence Kersta called voiceprints. The spectrograms are graphs, with the frequency of the sounds shown on the vertical (side) axis and time shown on the horizontal (bottom) axis. The darkness of the lines reflects the intensity of the sounds. The top two spectrograms come from the same person, saying the same word in two different recording sessions. The bottom spectrogram shows the same word spoken by a different person. Supporters of voiceprint technology say that trained analysts can separate differences between voices from those in the same voice speaking at different times. (FBI)

under which the tape of the unknown voice was made. If the mystery voice was recorded over a telephone, for instance, the analyst will record suspects' voices through a telephone line as well. The tester will ask the suspects to repeat the exact words spoken in the crime-related tape. The suspects will be told to say the words several times, so that the analyst can see the range of variations in each individual's voice.

Police can obtain a court order to make a suspect provide a voice recording. Under some circumstances, however, they may want to record a suspect's voice without that person's knowledge. They may tap the person's telephone, for example, or have an informant or undercover officer wear a "wire" (secret recording device) while talking to him or her. In this case, the person speaking to the suspect must persuade the suspect to say as many of the words in the crime-related sample as possible. Here, as with a poorly recorded or disguised unknown voice, a long sample of speech will be needed for accurate analysis.

Analyzing Spectrograms

A modern voice analyst uses both ears and eyes in trying to determine whether two voice samples match. The analyst first listens to the two tapes repeatedly, trying to detect similarities and differences in the way the voices make single sounds and groups of sounds, the way breathing interacts with the sounds, and unusual speech habits, inflections, and accents. To make comparison easier, the analyst usually rerecords several examples of selected speech sounds from the unknown and suspect tapes in alternating order and listens to them again. The analyst then visually compares spectrogram tracings of the same speech sounds made by the unknown voice and by the suspect or suspects, looking for similarities and differences in the frequencies of fundamentals and harmonics and in loudness.

At the end of the examination, the analyst reaches one of five conclusions: The samples definitely match, the samples probably match, the samples probably do not match, the samples definitely do not match, or the test was inconclusive. An analyst must find 20 points of similarity and no unexplainable differences in order to declare a definite match. A definite nonmatch requires 20 or more differences between the two tapes.

How Accurate Is Voice Identification?

Different researchers have reached very different conclusions about the accuracy of spectrographic voice identification. Experienced spectrographic analyst Tom Owen told Katherine Ramsland in an interview reprinted in Court TV's online crime library, "When you're comparing a known and an unknown voice using a verbatim exemplar [both voices speaking exactly the same words], there are no errors." On the other hand, Jonas Lindh of the department of linguistics at Göteborg University in Sweden claimed in a 2004 paper, "Several experiments have shown that spectrograms are not reliable to verify identity."

As with the polygraph ("lie detector"), researchers agree that most problems with sound spectrography's accuracy lie, not with the machines or even the recordings, but with the human beings who analyze them and the techniques used to determine matches and nonmatches. Katherine Ramsland writes in her series of articles about Voiceprints in the Court TV online crime library, "All of the studies that have been done on spectrographic accuracy, including a 1986 FBI survey, show that those people who have been properly trained and who use standard aural and visual procedures get highly accurate results. The opposite is true where training and/or analysis methods are limited." Proper training, Ramsland says, consists of two to four weeks of classes in spectrographic analysis, followed by a two-year internship period in which at least 100 of the person's analyses are checked by experienced analysts, and, finally, an examination given by a board of experts in the field.

"Voiceprint" analysis, like polygraph testing, is still controversial, and it is likely to remain so for the foreseeable future. T. R. O'Connor, a professor at North Carolina Wesleyan College, states in notes for his criminal investigation course, "The scientific community, on [the] whole, hasn't exactly warmed up to the idea of spectrographic voice recognition." Nonetheless, many large police departments own sound spectrographs or hire consultants to perform spectrographic analysis. The CIA, FBI, and other intelligence agencies use voice recognition in attempts to identify terrorists. Voice analyst Steve Cain calls the technology "a very important tool in the arsenal against crime."

Chronology

1867	Melville Bell creates system of symbols to represent spoken sounds visually
1902	Lawrence G. Kersta born in New Jersey
1930s	Late in the decade, Kersta begins working for Bell Telephone Laboratories
1941	Kersta and other engineers at Bell Laboratories create sound spectrograph, or automatic sound analyzer, for possible military use during World War II
1960	At request of New York police, Kersta creates an improved sound spectrograph
1962	Kersta publishes article in *Nature* describing research on 50,000 voices and claiming that each voice produces unique spectrograms
1964	Kersta leaves Bell Laboratories and establishes Voiceprint Laboratories Corporation
1966	Michigan state police set up voice identification unit and hire Kersta to train officers to use his machines and analyze spectrograms
1967	Sound spectrograph evidence first used in a trial
late 1960s, 1970s	Kersta travels around world to demonstrate sound spectrograph
	Many courts refuse to allow sound spectrograph evidence in trials because the technology is not accepted by the scientific community
1973	Kersta sells Voiceprint Laboratories to Rik Alexanderson
1995	Kersta dies in Miami, Florida

Further Reading

Books

Evans, Colin. *Murder 2: The Second Casebook of Forensic Detection.* Hoboken, N.J.: Wiley, 2004.
    Contains a short chapter on voiceprints.

Articles

American Association for Artificial Intelligence. "Speech." Available online. URL: http://www.aaai.org/AITopics/html/speech.html. Accessed on December 8, 2005.
    Provides brief discussions of computer recognition and synthesis of speech, including numerous links to articles on the subject.

Kersta, L. G. "Voiceprint Identification." *Nature* 196 (1962): 1,253–1,257.
    Paper in which Kersta described two years of research on spectrographic voice identification.

Lindh, Jonas. "Handling the 'Voiceprint' Issue." Available online. URL: http://www.ling.su.se/fon/fonetik_2004/lindh_voiceprint_fonteik2004.pdf. Posted in 2004. Accessed on December 2, 2005.
    Scientific article that reviews research on spectrographic voice identification and concludes that the technique is unreliable and has not been accepted by the scientific community.

McDermott, Michael C., and Tom Owen. "Voice Identification: The Aural/Spectrographic Method." Available online. URL: http://www.owlinvestigations.com/forensic_articles/aural_spectrographic/fulltext.html. Accessed on November 29, 2005.
    Extensive article by two experienced spectrographic analysts covers the history of voice identification, the sound spectrograph, the techniques by which voices are identified, standards for admission of spectrographic evidence in court, and research studies on the method's accuracy.

O'Connor, T. R. "Spectrographic Voice Recognition." Available online. URL: http://faculty.ncwc.edu/toconnor/315/315lect09c.htm. Last updated December 20, 2004. Accessed on September 24, 2005.
    Class notes by a professor at North Carolina Wesleyan College briefly describing the history and technology of spectrographic voice recognition.

Ramsland, Katherine. "Voiceprints." Available online. URL: http:// www.crimelibrary.com/criminal_mind/forensics/voiceprints/1. html. Accessed on September 22, 2005.
Series of articles, part of Court TV's crime library, that describes voiceprint technology, the way judges have viewed it, and its use in several court cases.

8
BONE BIOGRAPHIES

CLYDE SNOW AND FORENSIC ANTHROPOLOGY

Identifying a freshly dead body usually is not difficult. Facial features, hair color, and fingerprints provide clues. If a body has been dead for months, years, or decades, however, only a skeleton may be left—or perhaps just a handful of bones. Faced with mere bones, even an experienced medical examiner may have trouble figuring out who left them behind. In such a case, he or she often asks for the help of a "bone detective"—a forensic anthropologist such as Clyde Snow.

Anthropologists study humans and other primates (monkeys and apes), especially the ways in which human or other groups differ from one another. Physical anthropologists study physical differences. Forensic anthropologists are physical anthropologists who apply their knowledge of human differences, especially differences in bones, to investigation of crimes and other legal matters.

Forensic anthropology has been recognized as a specialty within forensic science only since the early 1970s. Interest in the field has increased greatly in recent years, but even today, only about 150 forensic anthropologists work in the United States. Clyde Snow is one of the best known of these, thanks to his work in revealing the fate of thousands of people killed by repressive governments. "Bones make good witnesses," Snow's profile in the 1997 *Current Biography Yearbook* quotes him as saying. "Although they speak softly, they never lie and they never forget."

Clyde Snow is one of the most famous modern forensic anthropologists. He has identified the bones of victims of air crashes, mass murderers, and repressive governments. (Daniel Hernandez)

Sampling Careers

Clyde Collins Snow grew up with a firsthand view of life and death. Born in Fort Worth, Texas, on January 7, 1928, to Wister Clyde and Sarah Isabel Snow, Clyde—called "Sonny" as a child—grew up in the tiny town of Ralls, Texas. He often went with his father, a country doctor, to visit patients on their farms and ranches in the dry Texas Panhandle. During these trips, Sonny Snow saw babies being born and sick people dying.

W. C., as most people called the doctor, had never heard of forensic anthropology, but Sonny Snow saw his father perform a simple version of a forensic anthropologist's job when Sonny was only 12 years old. During a hunting trip in New Mexico, the two met other hunters who had just found a pile of bones lying in the woods. When the hunters took W. C., Sonny, and a local deputy sheriff to the spot, W. C. examined the bones and said that some were human, while others belonged to a deer. He guessed that the dead man had been a hunter who shot a deer, tried to drag the animal's heavy body back to his car, and had a fatal heart attack in the process.

As Clyde Snow grew up, he showed little interest in following in the footsteps of his hardworking father. Clyde was expelled from high school for a prank with firecrackers. His parents sent him to the New Mexico Military Institute in Roswell, and he did poorly there as well until a roommate taught him how to study. Snow graduated from the institute with an Associate of Arts degree in 1947.

Snow enrolled in Southern Methodist University in Dallas, but he cared more about parties than about homework and soon flunked out. After an equally uninspiring performance at several other schools, he entered Eastern New Mexico University in Portales, one of the few colleges that would accept him. He earned a B.S. from that university in 1951.

Still undecided about what career to follow, Snow began a master's degree program in zoology at Texas Technical University in Lubbock. He left a year later to attend medical school at Baylor University in Houston, then returned to the Texas Tech program after another two years. He earned a M.S. in zoology from Texas Tech in 1955. After that, he spent three years in the U.S. Air Force (USAF) Medical Service Corps at the USAF Histopathology Center, part of Lackland Air Force Base in Texas. (Histopathology is the study of diseased tissue under a microscope.)

Snow started doctoral work in archaeology at the University of Arizona in 1958. Archaeologists study tools, buildings, and other artifacts left behind by earlier civilizations. Snow learned these scientists' careful way of working, which has much in common with the way forensic scientists or criminalists investigate a crime scene. Archaeologists divide a site into small, numbered squares and then slowly excavate each square, using trowels, spoons, and even toothbrushes. When they find an artifact, they write down the number of the square where the object is located and note how deep within the square it lies. They photograph the artifact in place, to show its exact position, before removing it.

Archaeology as a profession did not hold Snow's interest, so he changed his major to anthropology. He studied monkeys in Puerto Rico and, for his Ph.D. project, tracked the growth and development of African savanna baboons. He earned his Ph.D. in 1967.

The Stories Bones Tell

Long before Clyde Snow completed his study on baboons, he had turned his attention to humans. In 1960, he joined the physical anthropology laboratory of the Civil Aeromedical Institute (CAMI) in Oklahoma City, part of the Federal Aviation Administration's Aeronautical Center. (He became head of the laboratory in 1968.) He also began teaching physical anthropology at the University of Oklahoma, Norman, in 1962.

HUMAN SKELETON

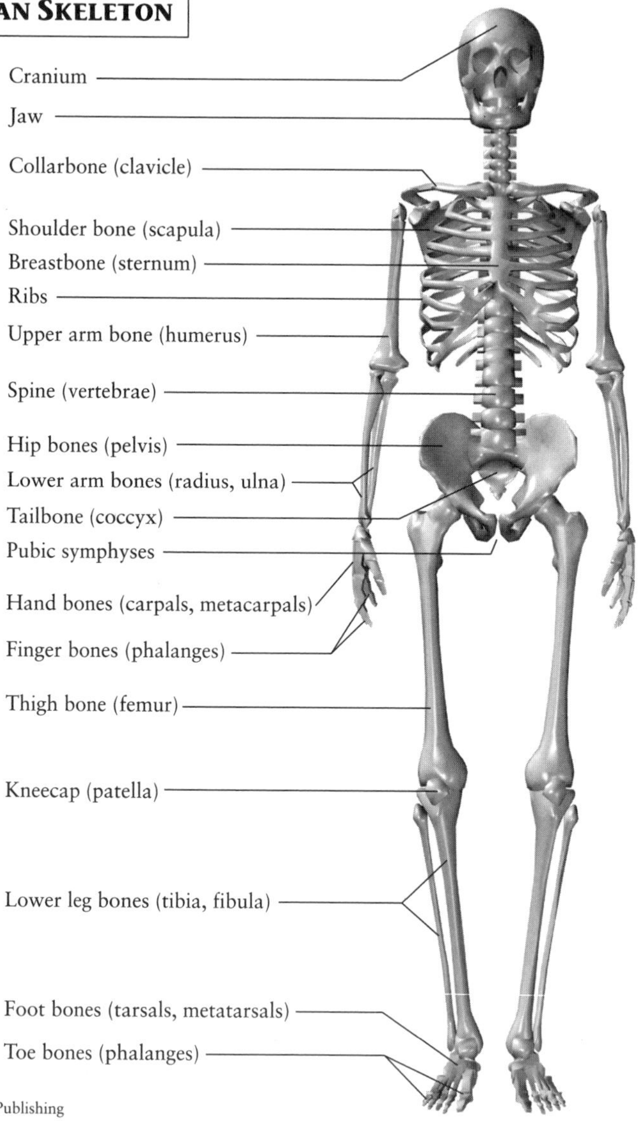

Cranium

Jaw

Collarbone (clavicle)

Shoulder bone (scapula)
Breastbone (sternum)
Ribs
Upper arm bone (humerus)

Spine (vertebrae)

Hip bones (pelvis)
Lower arm bones (radius, ulna)
Tailbone (coccyx)
Pubic symphyses

Hand bones (carpals, metacarpals)

Finger bones (phalanges)

Thigh bone (femur)

Kneecap (patella)

Lower leg bones (tibia, fibula)

Foot bones (tarsals, metatarsals)
Toe bones (phalanges)

© Infobase Publishing

All the bones of the skeleton tell stories to forensic anthropologists such as Clyde Snow. Examining and measuring certain bones can reveal a dead person's height (stature), age, sex, and race. The skeleton can also provide information about a person's health and activities.

Snow's job at CAMI was to study the way the human body interacts with aircraft and related equipment in order to increase air safety. Much of his work focused on plane crashes. Because he often had to try to identify bodies that had been torn apart or badly burned in these disasters, Snow learned how to determine people's height (stature), sex (gender), race, and age by studying their bones. Pioneer physical anthropologists had worked out techniques for doing this, beginning in the late 19th century.

Determining sex was often the easiest task, Snow found. The bones that show gender differences most clearly are those of the pelvis—the hip bones. Women's pelvises are wider, to permit the passage of babies during birth, and lower. Men's arm and leg bones also are usually longer and heavier than women's. Men's skulls have more noticeable brow ridges than the skulls of women.

Differences in the bones of the face can suggest a person's racial group. For instance, the bony ridge at the bottom of the nose is usually higher in Caucasoids than in other races. Negroids have wider nasal cavities and a larger gap between the eyes than other groups. The margins of the nasal cavity are often smoother in Mongoloids (people of Asian descent).

Age is more difficult to determine, but certain bones can be used as rough clocks. The best clock is the pubic symphyses, the parts of the two hip bones that meet in the front of the pelvis. Scientists found that the shape and texture of these areas change in a predictable way during a person's life. The cranium, or upper part of the skull, can also show age. Zigzag lines called sutures, which connect the bones of the cranium, become narrower and harder as a child grows to adulthood. Hard outgrowths on the bones of the spine (vertebrae) and some other bones, as well as wear on joints, are signs of a relatively old person.

Snow could figure out stature by measuring the long bones of the legs and arms. He fed these measurements into a mathematical formula, then looked up the stature in tables that were developed in the late 19th century and revised in the 1940s and 1950s. (Today Snow and other forensic anthropologists simply type their measurements into a computer, and the computer performs the calculations and looks up the stature for them.) He could also tell whether a person was right- or left-handed because the bones of the arm that the person used the most were slightly longer than the bones of the other arm.

Snow learned that teeth are among the most valuable bones for final identification. Fillings or unusual features, such as a chipped tooth or a gap between the front teeth, can be checked against dental X-rays made before death. Marks on other bones, such as healed breaks or scarring left by disease, are also useful if a missing person's medical records can be obtained for comparison. All these features of bone together make up what Snow calls a person's *osteobiography*—"a brief but very useful and informative biography of an individual contained within the skeleton," as he terms it in Colin Evans's book *Murder 2*.

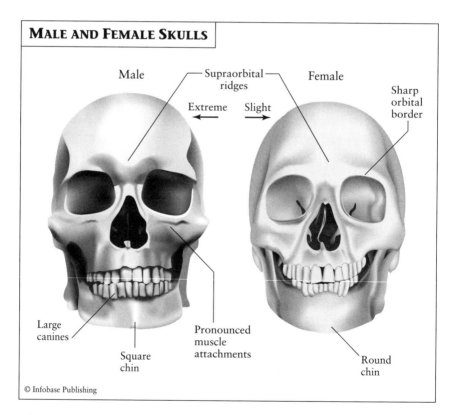

MALE AND FEMALE SKULLS

Male — Supraorbital ridges — Female

Extreme   Slight

Sharp orbital border

Large canines

Square chin

Pronounced muscle attachments

Round chin

© Infobase Publishing

This diagram shows some of the differences that reveal whether a skull belonged to a man or a woman.

SOLVING PROBLEMS: MEASURING BONES

Two French scientists and one German scientist measured hundreds of skeletons in the 1890s to prepare the tables that physical anthropologists in the early 20th century used to determine stature from measurements of arm and leg bones. While using these tables in a depressing task for the U.S. government just after World War II, Mildred Trotter, a teacher of anatomy at the Washington University School of Medicine in St. Louis, Missouri, came to realize that the tables were no longer accurate.

The army's Graves Registration Service hired Trotter and other physical anthropologists in the late 1940s to identify the remains of soldiers killed in the war. As Clyde Snow and others would do later, Trotter used medical records, X-ray photographs, dental charts, and other information to give names to the bones sent to her at a morgue in Hawaii. After she made the identifications, she found that the men's height, as given in their military records, often differed by an inch or two from the figures she had arrived at by using the European tables.

Trotter realized that the tables needed to be revised because bodies had changed. Better food and health care had made people taller, on average, than they had been 50 years before. North Americans also differed from Europeans in some measurements. To the irritation of her military superiors, Trotter and her assistants began measuring the arm and leg bones of hundreds of skeletons that they had already identified. Using these measurements combined with the men's true height, she prepared new tables and rewrote the equation used to determine stature.

About six years later, the Korean War offered a second grim opportunity to improve anthropologists' power to read biographies in bones. Most U.S. soldiers in World War II had been Caucasian, but a wider variety of ethnic groups fought in the Korean War. Again working for the Graves Registration Service, Trotter revised her tables once more to include measurements from these groups.

Another physical anthropologist, T. Dale Stewart of the Smithsonian Institution, took similar advantage of work for the army to check and revise assumptions about the way bones change with age. He and a coworker, Thomas McKern, developed a formula for determining age on the basis of the degree to which certain bones have joined together. The tables and formulas that Trotter and Stewart created are still used.

The Flight 191 Disaster

Snow's skill in reading "osteobiographies" was put to one of its greatest tests in 1979, when he helped to identify the burned and shattered remains of 273 people who died in the fiery crash of American Airlines flight 191. The DC-10 aircraft lost an engine and part of a wing and fell to the ground minutes after taking off from Chicago's O'Hare Airport on May 25, producing the worst airline disaster in U.S. history up to that time. The remains of the crash victims—10,000 to 12,000 different pieces—were mixed together and scattered over a wide area.

In a huge airplane hangar converted into a morgue, about 100 investigators took on the grisly task of trying to match the body parts and determine the passenger to whom each set belonged. The team found names for most of the dead within a few days, but about 50 bodies or body parts remained unidentified. At the request of the Cook County medical examiner, Snow flew to Chicago and spent five weeks trying to solve these remaining puzzles. In Snow's 1997 *Current Biography* profile, he called this the most unpleasant experience of his life.

Snow found one way to make the grim work a little easier. He and a computer programmer from American Airlines designed software that helped to match information about body parts, such as bone measurements and X-rays, with information about passengers supplied by relatives and doctors. Given facts about a body, the program called up descriptions of the 10 passengers that best fitted those statistics. Relatives were then questioned to produce a final identification from among those people. With the help of this program, Snow and other experts identified 20 bodies out of the mysterious 50.

Many forensic anthropologists have used Snow's program since that time. Snow himself applied it in 1995 to identify victims of the Oklahoma City terrorist bombing.

Putting a Face on Murder

As if handling the Flight 191 disaster was not enough, Snow also had to deal with a second set of bodies while he was in Chicago.

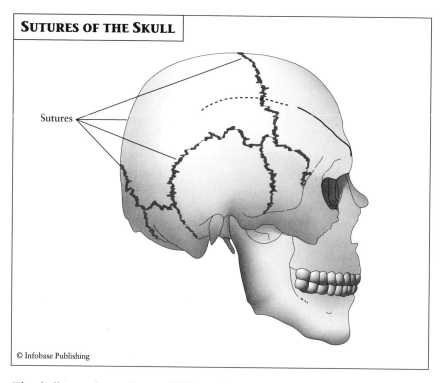

SUTURES OF THE SKULL

Sutures

© Infobase Publishing

The skull is made up of several different bones with jagged edges. The connections between the bones, called sutures, are wide and soft in children. They become narrower and harder as a child grows up, finally fusing into solid bone. Examining the sutures of a skull can help a forensic anthropologist determine the age of the skull's owner.

Unlike the victims of the air crash, these people had been killed deliberately.

By 1979, Clyde Snow was as familiar with murders as with air wrecks. Oklahoma City police had heard about his expertise soon after he began working for CAMI, and they started asking him to help them identify skeletons. As the 1960s advanced and Snow's reputation grew, police and medical examiners from farther away also consulted him.

In December 1978, pursuing a report of a missing young man, police had visited John Wayne Gacy, a contractor living in Des

Plaines, Illinois, and discovered a crawl space beneath Gacy's house packed with bodies and bones. Gacy told them that there were more skeletons under other parts of the house and garage. Detectives eventually found that Gacy had murdered at least 33 young men, making him the worst serial killer the United States had known up to that time.

Gacy said he did not remember the names of most of the men he had killed. Police learned the identities of some, but others remained a mystery. Identifying the bodies was difficult because Gacy had piled them on top of one another, so the bones mixed together. All the bodies, furthermore, belonged to people of the same gender and about the same age.

While working with Snow on the Flight 191 crash, Robert Stein, the Cook County medical examiner, asked Snow to look at the bodies of 14 of Gacy's victims who were still unidentified. Snow and radiologist (X-ray specialist) John Fitzpatrick found the names of five more of the young men later in 1979. For help with the rest, Snow turned to Betty Pat Gatliff, a medical artist with whom he had worked many times before.

Gatliff's specialty is facial reconstruction—sculpting faces on skulls to create likenesses that relatives might recognize. (She calls her studio the "SKULLpture Lab.") She began to put faces on the murdered men by gluing pencil erasers, cut to different heights, onto the fronts of their skulls. She determined the heights by looking at tables that Wilhelm His, a German anatomist, had developed in 1895. The figures are about the same for all people; differences in faces depend on differences in skulls, not on variations in the muscles and skin that cover them.

Gatliff put artificial flesh on her faces by laying strips of clay around the erasers. She completed the sculptures with false eyes, teeth, and wigs if the victims' hair color was known. Pictures of her sculptures were broadcast on television and printed in newspapers. Her work did not produce identifications for any more of Gacy's victims, unfortunately, but she has been successful in other cases. "She has . . . reconstructed hundreds of faces, often with near-photographic accuracy," Snow wrote in *Sciences* in 1995.

Identifying the "Angel of Death"

Clyde Snow left CAMI in 1980 to become a full-time consultant in forensic anthropology. He worked on one of his most important cases in June 1985, when he and other experts were called to São Paulo, Brazil, to try to determine whether a skeleton removed from a cemetery in nearby Embú belonged to one of the most notorious mass murderers of all time: Josef Mengele, nicknamed the "Angel of Death."

Mengele, a physician, had headed the infamous Nazi German extermination camp Auschwitz in Poland. Some 400,000 people, many of them Jews, were killed at Auschwitz in the early 1940s. Mengele personally tortured many of the camp's inmates or performed bizarre medical experiments on them.

Mengele escaped from Germany when the country was defeated at the end of World War II and, like some other Nazi leaders, fled to South America. He lived in several different countries before settling in Brazil in 1961. He stayed there under a false name until 1979, when he drowned accidentally at the age of 67. German friends buried him at Embú.

In early 1985, a tipster told police that the body at Embú belonged to Mengele. Determining the truth of this claim was important because some concentration camp survivors and relatives of others who had died there still hoped to capture the Nazi doctor alive and punish him for his crimes.

The team of scientists who met in São Paulo faced a difficult task. They had no X-rays or dental records from Mengele's years in Brazil to compare with the bones they were given. Their only information about Mengele's appearance came from a few photographs and records made by the SS, the German secret police, of which the physician had been a member.

The forensic experts quickly agreed that the Embú skeleton came from a male of the same race and height as Mengele. The bones also suggested a man of the age that Mengele would have been in 1979. With further examination, the group found features that matched what they knew of Mengele, including a gap between the skull's front teeth (shown strikingly in photographs of the physician) and a healed hip fracture that could have come from a motorcycle accident that Mengele suffered in 1942. Still, the identification was far from certain.

Richard Helmer, a German specialist on the team, provided the most convincing evidence that the skeleton was Mengele's by using a technique called skull-face superposition. Like Betty Pat Gatliff preparing to make a facial reconstruction sculpture, Helmer looked at tables showing the thickness of skin and muscle above 30 different points on a skull. He then used clay to attach pins to the Embú skull at those points. On each pin he placed a white marker showing the height above the skull that the skin at that spot would have reached when the skull's owner was alive.

Helmer mounted the skull, now looking like a bizarre pincushion, on an aluminum post. He put a photograph of Mengele on another post and adjusted high-resolution video cameras until images of

Excavating skeletons from graves is often part of a forensic anthropologist's job. The diggers shown here are from the FBI, but Clyde Snow and his students have done similar work at mass graves in countries around the world. (FBI)

the skull and photo were the same size. Using a video processor, he placed one image on top of the other and looked at both together on a television screen. At each point, the skin on the photograph lined up exactly with the white markers on the pins.

Putting all their findings together, Clyde Snow and the other forensic experts concluded that "within a reasonable scientific certainty," the body that had been buried at Embú was Mengele's. About a year later, German investigators discovered a dentist who had treated Mengele in the late 1970s, and the dentist gave them Mengele's dental X-rays. These, too, fit the Embú skull. Few people now doubted that the man who had drowned in 1979 was Josef Mengele. The Angel of Death was really dead.

The Disappeared

The discovery of Josef Mengele's remains made headlines around the world, but Clyde Snow saw his work on the Mengele case merely as a break from a job that he felt was far more important: putting names to hundreds of victims of a more recent dictatorship who were buried in mass graves in Argentina.

Snow's work in Argentina began soon after that country changed governments in December 1983. A military regime had controlled Argentina between 1976 and 1983, forbidding all forms of political dissent. During what the government called the "dirty war," soldiers and police kidnapped thousands of citizens, imprisoning them without trial and frequently torturing and killing them as well. In most cases, the people's relatives were never told what had happened to them. These people—up to 20,000 of them—were known simply as *los desaparecidos,* "the disappeared."

As one of his first acts in office, Argentine president Raúl Alfonsín appointed a commission to investigate the fate of the disappeared. Many of these executed citizens were thought to have been buried in mass graves near the detention centers to which police had taken kidnapped people. Bodies disposed of in this way were listed in cemetery records only as "N.N.," short for "no name" in Spanish. Alfonsín's commission asked the American Association for the Advancement of Science (AAAS) to send forensic scientists to help

Argentine officials identify the remains in the mass graves. Clyde Snow was one of the experts whom the AAAS contacted. Snow made his first trip to Argentina in June 1984. A local judge gave him permission to exhume and analyze a sample body, but he found that no Argentine forensic scientists or archaeologists would help him. Many citizens thought the military government might soon return to power, and they feared that if they cooperated with outsiders, they in turn would "disappear."

Unable to find professionals, Snow turned to students. Morris Tidball Binz, an Argentine medical student who had met Snow at a lecture, recruited five friends to help the anthropologist carry out the exhumation. Although these young men and women had studied anthropology and archaeology, none had ever dug up a buried body or identified a skeleton before. Snow showed them how to excavate a grave slowly and systematically, as an archaeologist would, and how to read osteobiographies. Christopher Joyce and Eric Stover write in *Witnesses from the Grave* that Snow also taught his new helpers how to handle the wrenching emotions they were sure to feel when they identified the remains of young people like themselves—possibly even people they had known. "Do your work in the daytime," Snow said. "Cry at night."

Seeking Justice

In April 1985, after several months of exhuming bodies of the "disappeared" with his student group, Clyde Snow testified in the murder trial of nine former leaders of the Argentine military government. He told the court how his team had identified the bones of one young woman, Liliana Carmen Pereyra. Pereyra, a law student, had been 21 years old and five months pregnant when she was arrested in October 1977. Her bones showed that she had given birth, then was killed shortly afterward by a shotgun blast fired at close range.

According to a profile of Snow in *Current Biography Yearbook,* one judge later told Snow that the forensic anthropologist's testimony had helped him realize that the dictatorship's victims were not "paper people" but "at one time . . . flesh and blood." The court convicted five of the nine men and sentenced them to long terms

I WAS THERE: THE STUDENTS' FIRST BODY

In *Witnesses from the Grave*, Christopher Joyce and Eric Stover quote Clyde Snow's memories of his first graveside work with the Argentine student group. The digging began about nine A.M. at the Boulogne Cemetery in San Isidro, a suburb of Buenos Aires. Snow recalled:

> *The local judge was out there. And his secretaries, a couple of male lawyers. And the relatives of the deceased. That shocked me. We don't let relations within five miles of an exhumation in the United States. And there were high-level policemen, three guys in navy blue suits. . . . And there were spectators. And gravediggers.*
>
> *So here come these five frightened kids [one of the six students did not take part in this exhumation]. . . . The kids are scared to death because the police are out there. I'm scared to death because I don't know what I'm doing.*

None of the students except possibly Sergio Aleksandrovic, an archaeology major, had ever excavated a site, let alone a grave. Snow showed the team how to dig a test probe to determine how deep the body was buried. He then had gravediggers remove the soil down to a level about four inches (10 cm) above the remains. He and the students placed wooden planks across the open hole. They lay on the planks and began scraping away the remaining earth with trowels and spoons.

In late morning, the moment that Snow had been dreading arrived: The group uncovered the body's skull. The jaws of the skull hung open, as if in a silent scream. "There was a bullet hole right up over the eye," Snow told Joyce and Stover. "There was an earthworm right next to it. This was the first *desaparecido* that the kids had ever seen. I didn't know what they were going to do."

One of the students, Patricia Bernardi, abruptly set down her trowel and walked away. Snow was not sure she would ever come back. At first only Morris Tidball Binz, who had seen corpses before in his medical studies, kept digging, but the remaining students soon reluctantly joined him.

Ten minutes passed. Then, as suddenly as she had left, Bernardi returned. Her eyes were red, but she seemed calm. Without a word, she picked up her trowel and went back to work.

in prison. In fact, however, their "prisons" proved to be luxury accommodations, and a few years later, the men were pardoned and released.

Even if his work could not bring the killers of the disappeared to justice, Snow felt that it was important to remind the world what repressive governments could do. He returned to Argentina several times during the 1980s to carry out more exhumations and continue training his increasingly expert group, which in 1986 took the title of Equipo Argentino de Antropología Forense (Argentine Forensic Anthropology Team). He also helped to establish an Argentine national forensic science center.

Mass Graves around the World

Other governments looked admiringly at what Snow and his team were accomplishing in Argentina. In the late 1980s and 1990s, he and the Argentine group were asked to investigate similar atrocities in the Philippines, Guatemala, Bolivia, Chile, Sri Lanka, Iraq, and the Congos. Their most widely publicized excavation took place in September 1996, as part of a United Nations war-crimes tribunal's investigation of events in what had been Yugoslavia. The team dug out part of a mass grave near the town of Vukovar. Serb soldiers had kidnapped some 200 Croatian Muslims from a local hospital, executed them, and buried them in this grave in November 1991. In an article in the March 1997 *Smithsonian*, Eric Stover, head of the Human Rights Center at the University of California, Berkeley, wrote that this excavation "soon developed into the largest forensic investigation of war crimes—or possibly of any crime—in history."

"Of all the forms of murder, none is more monstrous than that committed by a state against its own citizens," Clyde Snow said in a speech at a meeting of the American Association for the Advancement of Science in May 1984, just before he began his work in Argentina. "The great mass murderers of our time have accounted for no more than a few hundred victims. In contrast, states that have chosen to murder their own citizens can usually count their victims by the carload lot."

However, Snow added, "The homicidal state shares one trait with the solitary killer—like all murderers, it trips on its own egotism and drops a trail of clues which, when properly collected, preserved, and analyzed are as damning as a signed confession left in the grave. . . . Maybe it's time for the forensic scientists of the world to heed the old call of our favorite fictional prototype [Sherlock Holmes]: 'Quick, Watson, the game's afoot!'—and go after the biggest game of all." By revealing the victims of government mass murder, Snow explained, forensic anthropologists not only would bring peace to the victims' relatives but also might discourage other governments from committing similar crimes. In the game of hunting government murderers, as in the game of tracking down individual killers and identifying their victims, Clyde Snow knows no peer.

Chronology

1890s	European scientists develop tables for determining stature from measurements of long bones and for showing the thickness of skin and muscle in faces
1928	Clyde Collins Snow born in Fort Worth, Texas, on January 7
1940s, 1950s	U.S. scientists revise physical anthropology tables after measuring bones of war dead
1947	Snow earns Associate of Arts degree from New Mexico Military Institute
1951	Snow earns B.S. from Eastern New Mexico University
1955	Snow earns M.S. in zoology from Texas Technical University
1955–58	Snow serves in U.S. Air Force (USAF) Medical Service Corps at USAF Histopathology Center
1960	Snow joins physical anthropology laboratory of the Federal Aviation Administration's Civil Aeromedical Institute (CAMI) and begins studying air crashes
1962	Snow begins teaching physical anthropology at University of Oklahoma, Norman

1960s	Police and medical examiners in Oklahoma City and, later, elsewhere ask Snow for help in identifying skeletons
1967	Snow earns Ph.D. in anthropology from University of Arizona
1968	Snow becomes head of physical anthropology laboratory at CAMI
1978	In December, police in Des Plaines, Illinois, find remains of 33 young men under the house of contractor John Wayne Gacy, who confesses to murdering them
1979	On May 25, American Airlines flight 191 crashes soon after takeoff from Chicago's O'Hare Airport, killing 273 people; Snow, among others, is asked to help in identifying the scattered remains; he develops a computer program to speed up the task
	Snow identifies five of the men Gacy killed
	The man later proved to be Josef Mengele, former head of the Auschwitz extermination camp in Poland, drowns accidentally in Brazil
1980	At Snow's request, Betty Ann Gatliff makes sculptures of Gacy's remaining nine victims
	Snow leaves CAMI to become a full-time consultant in forensic anthropology
1983	In December, after the first free election in 11 years, Raúl Alfonsín's government assumes power in Argentina; Alfonsín appoints a commission to investigate the fate of thousands of people made to "disappear" by the former military government; the commission asks the American Association for the Advancement of Science (AAAS) to send experts to help local officials exhume mass graves and identify victims
1984	At the request of the AAAS, Snow visits Argentina for the first time in June; he recruits a student group to help with exhumation
1985	Snow testifies in April at the trial of nine former leaders of the Argentine military government; five of the men are found guilty of murder

In June, Snow and other experts go to Brazil to examine a skeleton reputed to have belonged to Nazi mass murderer Josef Mengele and conclude "within a reasonable scientific certainty" that the bones are Mengele's

1986	German investigators obtain Mengele's dental X-rays and show that these match the remains found in Brazil
late 1980s, 1990s	Snow and his Argentine team investigate government mass murder in several countries
1995	Snow uses computer program to identify victims of terrorist bombing in Oklahoma City
1996	In September, Snow and the Argentine group excavate part of a mass grave near Vukovar, in the former Yugoslavia, as part of a United Nations war-crimes investigation

Further Reading

Books

Evans, Colin. *The Casebook of Forensic Detection: How Science Solved 100 of the World's Most Baffling Crimes.* Hoboken, N.J.: Wiley, 1996.
> Includes short chapters on Snow's identification of the victims of John Wayne Gacy and of the skeleton of Josef Mengele in Brazil.

———. *Murder 2: The Second Casebook of Forensic Detection.* Hoboken, N.J.: Wiley, 2004.
> Includes short chapters on Snow and on his discovery of the identity of Oklahoma outlaw Elmer McCurdy.

Fridell, Ron. *Solving Crimes: Pioneers of Forensic Science.* New York: Franklin Watts, 2000.
> For young adults. Includes a chapter on Clyde Snow.

Joyce, Christopher, and Eric Stover. *Witnesses from the Grave: The Stories Bones Tell.* Boston: Little, Brown, 1991.
> Describes Clyde Snow's career in forensic anthropology, especially his work in exposing mass murders committed by governments such as the military regime in Argentina. Includes two chapters on the history of forensic anthropology as well as background on Snow.

Articles

Guntzel, Jeff. "'The Bones Don't Lie': Forensic Anthropologist Clyde Snow Travels Continents to Bring the Crimes of Mass Murderers to Light." *National Catholic Reporter* 40 (July 30, 2004): 13–16.

> Recounts the work of Snow and the Argentine Forensic Anthropology Team in excavating mass graves and revealing human rights abuses in many countries.

Hanson, Doug. "Body of Evidence: The Dead Man's Story." *Law Enforcement Technology* 32 (July 2005): 58–64.

> Explains the work of forensic anthropologists, including techniques for identifying bodies and determining cause of death.

Huyghe, Patrick. "No Bone Unturned." *Discover* 9 (December 1988): 39–45.

> Describes Clyde Snow's most famous cases.

Snow, Clyde. "Murder Most Foul." *Sciences* 35 (May–June 1995): 16–20.

> Tells how the author and other forensic anthropologists investigated mass murders and human rights violations in a variety of countries.

"Snow, Clyde Collins." In *Current Biography Yearbook 1997.* New York: H. W. Wilson, 1997.

> Describes Snow's life and career up to 1997, based on profiles published in magazines and newspapers.

Stover, Eric. "The Grave at Vukovar." *Smithsonian* 27 (March 1997): 40–51.

> Recounts Snow's excavation of a mass burial of more than 200 Croatian Muslims killed by Serbs near the Croatian city of Vukovar, in the former Yugoslavia, in September 1996.

University of Tennessee Forensic Anthropology Center. "What Is Forensic Anthropology?" Available online. URL: http://web.utk. edu/~anthrop/FACwhatis.html. Accessed on November 4, 2005.

> Briefly describes forensic anthropology, the kinds of work forensic anthropologists do in connection with crimes, and the training they receive.

Web Sites

Forensic Anthropology. University of Utah Health Sciences Center. URL: http://library.med.utah.edu/kw/osteo/forensics. Accessed on December 20, 2005.

Includes news stories about forensic anthropologists' contributions to human rights work and investigation of crimes, as well as explanations of the way forensic anthropologists determine age, sex, and stature (height) from bones.

Forensic Anthropology and Human Osteology Resources. ForensicAnthro.com. URL: http://www.forensicanthro.com. Accessed on September 22, 2005.

Includes answers to frequently asked questions about forensic anthropology and an extensive set of links to forensic anthropology resources for students (mostly for college-age and above).

THE BODY FARM

WILLIAM BASS AND DETERMINING TIME OF DEATH

Many forensic scientists do their work in antiseptic laboratories, far from the ugly realities of violent death. Even forensic anthropologists most commonly examine skeletons, little more disturbing than a Halloween prop. By contrast, the scientists at the University of Tennessee's Forensic Anthropology Center, formerly the Anthropological Research Facility (ARF), study forensic anthropology's least attractive subjects: as the center's founder, William M. Bass III, put it in *Death's Acre,* his autobiography, "bodies that are bloated, blasted, burned, buggy, rotted, sawed, gnawed, liquefied, mummified, or dismembered." Bass wrote that a visitor once suggested—only partly to honor him—that the facility's name be changed to the Bass Anthropological Research Facility (BARF). That nickname was never adopted, but another nickname was: Police detectives and mystery readers alike have come to know the Tennessee research center simply as the Body Farm.

The Forensic Anthropology Center may not be high on most scientists' lists of desirable places to work, but the information its researchers collect has brought many killers to justice. By showing exactly what happens to corpses under all kinds of conditions, day by day and hour by hour, the Body Farm's scientists help police determine when murder victims died. Suspects' accounts of their movements can be checked against that time to clear the innocent or point a finger at the guilty. "An accurate time-since-death estimate can make or break a murder case," Bass wrote in *Death's Acre.*

Hooked on Bones

William Bass himself had a painful encounter with death not long after he was born in Staunton, Virginia, on August 30, 1928. In March 1932, when Bass was just three and a half years old, his father, Marvin, an attorney, committed suicide. Bass's mother, Jennie, raised him. Death was far from Bass's mind when he enrolled in the University of Virginia in 1947. His major was psychology, and he graduated with a B.A. in that subject in 1951. He was then drafted into the military and spent three years at the Army Medical Research Laboratory in Fort Knox, Kentucky.

William Bass, a retired professor of physical anthropology at the University of Tennessee, Knoxville, established the university's Forensic Anthropology Center. The center, which studies how bodies break down after death, has been nicknamed the Body Farm. (William M. Bass and Photography Center, University of Tennessee)

When his military service was over, Bass returned to his plans for a career in psychology, beginning a master's degree program in counseling at the University of Kentucky, Lexington. Before long, however, he found his interests changing. Bass had taken a few anthropology courses while at the University of Virginia, and he took another during his first semester in graduate school. His professor in that class, Charles E. Snow, worked occasionally as a forensic anthropology consultant, and one day in April 1955, Snow asked Bass to come with him to identify the remains of a woman who had been killed in a car crash and fire several months before.

Bass wrote in *Death's Acre* that the woman's body was "burned, rotted, and waterlogged"—quite a change from the clean bone specimens that he and Snow's other students studied in their physical anthropology class. Far from feeling disgusted, however, Bass found his first forensic case "intellectually irresistible." He became so "hooked," as he put it, that he changed his focus of study to anthropology, especially forensic anthropology. He earned a master's degree in physical anthropology from the University of Kentucky in 1956.

Bass chose the University of Pennsylvania, Philadelphia, for his Ph.D. studies so he could work under Wilton Krogman, who had helped to found modern forensic anthropology in the 1940s and 1950s. Krogman became his mentor and close friend.

Ants Solve a Mystery

Unlike the corpses he encountered later at the Body Farm, the bodies William Bass studied during his first anthropology project had been dead for at least a hundred years. Beginning in 1957, Bass spent 14 summers in South Dakota examining the remains of the Arikara, a Native American people, as part of the Smithsonian River Basin Surveys, a research effort sponsored by the Smithsonian Institution. Bass excavated between 4,000 and 5,000 Indian burials during those years. In 1961, he earned his Ph.D. with a dissertation on prehistoric Plains Indians.

At first, Bass worked at what was known as the Sully site. He and the other anthropologists and archaeologists at the site had to make their excavations quickly because the entire area would soon be flooded by a new dam across the Missouri River. The archaeologists had found enough remains of the Arikara's earth-lodge houses to indicate that several hundred people had once lived at the site, but the scientists could not locate the spot where the village had buried its dead. The expedition leader asked Bass to solve this mystery.

Bass did so by using helpers that would later become essential in the Body Farm's work as well: insects. He noticed that ants around the site preferred to dig their anthills in places where the soil had been disturbed, because the loosened dirt made their task easier. This appeared to be true even when the disturbance had occurred long ago. Bass realized that digging graves would cause that kind of disruption, and he began to suspect that the ants could lead him to the lost Arikara burials.

Bass found that some of the prairie anthills contained small objects that the ants had found underground and brought to the surface to discard. Among these objects he spotted blue glass beads of a type that the Arikara were known to have used in jewelry, mixed with the tiny bones of human feet and fingers. Digging beneath groups of anthills that included such items, Bass and the students working under him discovered dozens of graves.

Inspiration from a Dead Cow

Bass joined the faculty of the University of Kansas, Lawrence, in September 1960 and remained there until 1971, eventually becoming a full professor. He also consulted for the Kansas Bureau of Investigation (KBI), usually helping to identify human skeletons that police or others discovered.

The case that gave Bass the beginning of the idea for the Body Farm did not involve human remains, however. In spring 1964, police found the recently butchered corpses of stolen cattle on the plains, and Harold Nye, the associate director of the KBI, asked Bass whether he could find out how long ago the animals had died by examining the skeleton of one of them. This information, Nye said, would help police determine which suspects might have committed the crime.

Bass had to admit that he could not do what the director wanted, as he reported in *Death's Acre*. "We do not know of any method by which you could tell the length of time since the cow has been killed," he wrote to Nye. "If you have some interested farmer who would be willing to kill a cow and let it lie, we could run an experiment on how long it would take for the flesh to decay and begin to build up some information in this area." Bass realized as he composed his letter that neither he nor anyone else knew much more about what happened to human bodies right after death than they did about cattle. The same sort of experiment that he had suggested for the cow might remedy that lack.

Bodies in a Barn

Bass moved to the Knoxville campus of the University of Tennessee in June 1971 to head the university's anthropology department. He was also appointed to be the first Tennessee state forensic anthropologist. That job naturally meant examining recently dead bodies, just as his work with the KBI had done—but examining a dead body in Tennessee, Bass soon learned, was more unpleasant than it had been in Kansas. Corpses tended to turn into leathery mummies in the dry soil of the prairie state, but in Tennessee, where the weather was hotter and more humid, bacteria and insects destroyed flesh quickly and messily.

At first, Bass kept the bodies from his police cases near his office at the university. After a janitor discovered a wrapped corpse in a mop closet and threatened to quit, however, Bass realized that he needed a storage spot far from living humans with sensitive noses. He asked the college dean for help, and the dean told him that he could have an empty pig barn on a farm belonging to the university's agricultural department. The farm was some distance outside Knoxville, so Bass and the dean did not expect its unsavory occupants to disturb anyone. Bass began using the deserted barn as his first anthropological research facility in 1972.

A Spectacular Mistake

Bass had forgotten about his Kansas cattle-rustling case soon after it occurred (Nye never carried out the experiment Bass had suggested), but a startling mistake the anthropologist made in early 1978 brought it to mind once more. The 1978 case began when a couple who lived near a small graveyard dating from the time of the Civil War (1861–65) called police to report that someone had tried to break open one of the coffins in the graveyard, probably looking for antique artifacts to steal and sell.

When officers visited the scene, they found that the desecrated grave belonged to Lieutenant Colonel William Shy. Shy's tombstone stated that he had died in the Battle of Nashville in 1864—yet what appeared to be a fresh body, still covered with flesh, was seated on Shy's damaged coffin. Strangely, the body lacked a head.

The coroner asked Bass to help the police identify the corpse, which they assumed was a murder victim that the criminals had dumped into Shy's grave. Bass examined the body and agreed that its owner had died recently, a year before at most. He was puzzled, however, to see that the body was dressed in a formal, old-fashioned black suit and white shirt, something like the clothes a waiter at an expensive restaurant might wear. Bass studied the body's bones further in his laboratory and decided that they had belonged to a man in his middle to late twenties, about five feet nine inches (1.8 m) tall.

Meanwhile, the police opened Shy's coffin and found more bones, including what was left of a skull. The skull had been shattered into 17 pieces by what Bass later called "a gunshot of enormous force," fired at close range. The skull fragments were free of flesh and colored brown, usually a sign of having been buried for many years. Bass found that many of the skull's teeth showed cavities, but none contained dental fillings.

As Bass uncovered these facts, he became more and more certain that he and the police had completely misunderstood the mysterious body. Rather than being the victim of a recent murder, the corpse was Colonel Shy himself, killed by an old-fashioned bullet of very large caliber during the Civil War battle. Instead of trying to push a fresh body into the half-opened coffin, the grave robbers had been attempting to pull the old one out. Shy's corpse had survived the passing decades so well because it had been embalmed—rare at the time, but not surprising for a wealthy and respected man—and placed in a sturdy, cast-iron coffin whose tight seals had kept insects and bacteria from invading the body. Investigators even tracked down a photograph of Shy, made several years before his death, that showed him wearing a suit just like the one on the corpse.

Founding the "Body Farm"

Colonel Shy was reburied after he was identified, but William Bass could not forget him. Bass felt that having been wrong by about 112 years in his first estimate of Shy's time of death was more than embarrassing. His mistake reminded him of the observation he had made 14 years before in the cattle rustling case: No one, not even forensic anthropologists, really knew much about the sequence of changes that dead bodies undergo as they pass from flesh-covered corpses to skeletons. That knowledge, he realized, could be vital in helping to solve murders and other crimes because it would allow the time of death to be determined precisely.

Bass decided that he and other anthropologists at the university should address that need. As he wrote in *Death's Acre:*

> We . . . [could] establish a research facility unlike any other in the world—a research facility that would systematically study human bodies by the dozens, ultimately by the hundreds; a laboratory where nature would be allowed to take its course with mortal flesh, under a variety of experimental conditions. At every step, scientists and graduate students would observe the processes, document variables such as temperature and humidity, and chart the timing of human decomposition.

Bass took his idea to the university chancellor. He needed a larger space than the land around the pig barn, he explained, and

William Bass and his students began clearing land for the Body Farm, then named the Anthropology Research Facility (ARF), near the University of Tennessee medical school in late 1980. (Dr. William M. Bass)

it should be close to the university so that he and his students could visit it without having to make a long drive each day. The chancellor said that Bass could have a vacant acre (0.4 ha) behind the university's medical school. Bass and his students began clearing the land in fall 1980.

Once Bass's group had their space, they needed bodies. Bass wrote to medical examiners and funeral directors around the state, asking for corpses that no one had claimed or that relatives were willing to donate. The team received its first donated body in May 1981, set it outside, and began to watch and take notes in what Bass described as "utter fascination."

The group named their plot of land the Anthropological Research Facility (ARF) in the early 1980s. Police and FBI agents, however, soon began calling it "the Body Farm." Bass and his students often found themselves using that term as well.

Parades of Insects

Bill Rodriguez, one of Bass's graduate students, carried out ARF's first major piece of research. Rodriguez painstakingly observed and photographed the parade of insects that help bodies break down. He found that although weather and other factors affect the timing of each species' arrival, the different species of insects always appear in the same order, or succession.

Large, shiny green flies called blowflies always arrive first, Rodriguez found—often only minutes after a corpse is placed outdoors if the weather is warm (flies cannot fly in cold weather). The female flies, already pregnant, lay their eggs in natural body openings or in wounds. Within hours, the eggs hatch into thousands of wormlike larvae, or maggots. The maggots, at first no bigger than grains of rice, feed and grow larger, eventually becoming about half an inch (1.27 cm) long. They then surrounded themselves with hard casings, inside which they transform into adult flies.

Rodriguez observed that yellow jackets, wasps, and ants appear almost as soon as the blowflies. Some of these insects nibble at the body, while others eat the fly eggs or newborn maggots. Later, as the blowfly maggots multiply, carrion beetles arrive. These beetles

THE INSECT PARADE

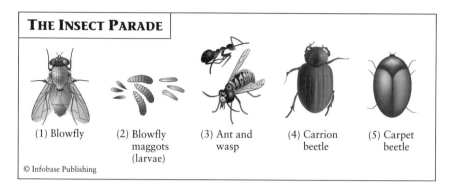

(1) Blowfly   (2) Blowfly   (3) Ant and   (4) Carrion   (5) Carpet
              maggots   wasp   beetle   beetle
              (larvae)

© Infobase Publishing

A parade of insects, always arriving in a certain order, helps break down bodies after death. Forensic entomologists can study the insects on a body to determine how long ago the body died. 1. Blowflies arrive first, within hours or even minutes of the time the body is placed in an open area. 2. The blowflies lay eggs on the body. A few hours later, the eggs hatch into wormlike larvae, or maggots. The maggots are about the size of a grain of rice at first, but later they may grow to half an inch (1.27 cm) in length. 3. Ants and wasps reach the body soon after the blowflies. 4. Carrion or carcass beetles come next, feeding on both the corpse and the blowfly eggs and maggots. 5. Carpet or dermestid beetles bring up the rear of the parade, arriving when the corpse is nearly reduced to a skeleton.

also eat both flesh and maggots. The last insects in the parade are dermestid beetles, sometimes called carpet beetles. They clean away the final shreds of tissue from what by now is an almost bare skeleton.

Rodriguez described his work in a scientific paper published in the *Journal of Forensic Sciences* in fall 1983. In *Death's Acre,* Bass notes proudly that, as what came to be known as "the first of the bug papers," Rodriguez's report became "one of the most heavily cited anthropology papers of all time." His research helped to found a new forensic anthropology specialty: forensic entomology, the study of insect involvement in murders or other criminal cases. If insects on and around a body are carefully collected, a forensic entomologist studying them can determine time of death to within five or six hours.

A Best Seller Brings Fame

The Anthropological Research Facility went on gathering knowledge about the breakdown of dead bodies during the 1980s and early 1990s. For example, Arpad Vass, another of Bass's students, recorded chemical changes that occur in the soil beneath a body laid or buried outdoors. Vass's work provided still another way of determining time of death.

The facility's staff grew and so did William Bass's reputation, both as a forensic scientist and as a teacher. In 1985, for example, the American Academy of Forensic Sciences gave him an award for outstanding contributions to forensic physical anthropology, and the Council for Advancement and Support of Education chose him as its National Professor of the Year.

Nonetheless, relatively few people had heard of the unusual research center in Tennessee until 1994, when writer Patricia Cornwell made a fictional version of the facility—and of Bass himself—a key part of her fifth mystery novel featuring forensic pathologist Kay Scarpetta. (A forensic pathologist specializes in disease and injury related to crimes and usually examines the flesh of a body. A forensic anthropologist such as William Bass or Clyde Snow, by contrast, concentrates on a body's bones.) Adopting the nickname that police and FBI agents had given to the facility, Cornwell called her book *The Body Farm.* Like her other mysteries, this one became a best seller—indeed, according to Bass, "one of the best-selling mysteries ever published."

Because of Cornwell's book, Bass and ARF suddenly found themselves famous. A stream of reporters demanded interviews, and dozens of groups, even including two dens of Cub Scouts, asked for tours of the facility. Some of the intrusions were distracting, but for the most part, Bass was pleased with the publicity the mystery produced. For one thing, it increased the Body Farm's supply of bodies. Some people chose to help scientific research by willing their bodies to ARF, and the more people who knew about the facility, the more donors it was likely to obtain.

Bass soon learned that not all publicity was good, however. In fall 1994, soon after Cornwell's book was published, a local television station learned that one of the homeless men whose corpses were given to the Body Farm had been a war veteran. The station aired a program accusing Bass and the Anthropological Research Facility of showing disrespect to veterans because of the way they used the body. Tennessee's commissioner of veterans' affairs saw the program and persuaded several members of the state legislature to introduce a bill that, if passed, would have prevented ARF from accepting unclaimed bodies. This would have severely hampered the scientists' research, Bass wrote in *Death's Acre*. Bass asked state law-enforcement officials for help in defeating the bill, and they persuaded the legislative committee reviewing the bill to let it drop.

A Kind of Immortality

William Bass and the other forensic anthropologists at ARF continued their work in the late 1990s. One of their chief projects was to develop still another technique that police could use to determine time since death. The method is based on the idea that bodies decompose faster in warm or humid weather than in cold, dry weather because heat and moisture make bacteria and insects more active. As Bass tells his students, "That's why you keep meat in the refrigerator, not in your kitchen cabinet."

Bass's technique figures in the effects of weather by determining what Bass calls accumulated degree days (ADDs). For example, 10 days with an average air temperature of 70 degrees amount to 700 ADDs, and so do 20 days with an average temperature of 35 degrees. Bass and his coworkers established a database showing a body's state of decomposition at each ADD.

To apply Bass's method, police check the database to determine the number of ADDs represented by the condition of a body they have found. They then ask local weather stations for daily temperatures in the crime scene area during the previous days or weeks. Once they know the ADDs and the temperatures, they can determine the number of days that have passed since the body's death and, therefore, the date on which the person died.

Bass retired from teaching in 1994 and from ARF in 1998, but the work of the Body Farm goes on. The facility expanded in June

---

SOLVING PROBLEMS: RESEARCH FOR A MYSTERY WRITER

Patricia Cornwell first contacted William Bass in the summer of 1993, when she was planning the novel that she later called *The Body Farm*. She explained that she planned to have her fictional killer leave the body of a victim in a basement for several days, then return and move the body elsewhere. What kinds of marks, she asked, might the body pick up during those days, and would it retain them in a new location? If he did not know the answers to these questions, could he possibly find out?

Medical examiners and detectives had sometimes asked Bass to perform special experiments for them, but an author had never done so before. Cornwell's questions interested Bass, and when he discussed them with a detective friend, the detective agreed that the answers might be useful to police as well. Bass therefore decided to carry out the experiment Cornwell had requested.

By luck, Bass had something like Cornwell's basement available: a concrete slab, recently added to the facility as the base for a new tool storage shed. He assembled a plywood enclosure, a little bigger than the body it would soon hold, and placed this box on top of the slab. To make the temperature in the box similar to that in the murderer's cool basement, he added an air conditioner, for which Cornwell paid.

The next body ARF received became a substitute for Cornwell's murder victim. Bass placed a penny (face up), a key, a small pair of scissors, and several other objects under various parts of the body. He then left it in the box for six days.

At the end of that time, Bass took the body to the morgue and examined it. The outline of the planted objects was plain to see on the body. For example, Bass wrote in *Death's Acre,* "Imprinted on the body's lower back was a perfect circle. Within the circle a faint imprint of Abraham Lincoln's head [from the penny] was clearly visible." The body had even picked up an unintended mark from a crack in the concrete beneath the corpse. Bass reported the results to Cornwell, giving her the information she needed to make her mystery true to life—or death.

1999 and changed its name to the Forensic Anthropology Center. Current research projects at the center include development of an "electronic nose" to analyze the molecules that produce the smells of decay. Center scientists hope to apply this information in training dogs to find dead bodies. In other experiments, facility scientists use ground-penetrating radar to locate bodies buried at different depths under soil or concrete. In addition to carrying on research, the center trains forensic anthropologists and gives courses to FBI agents and police.

Bodies given to the Body Farm achieve a kind of immortality, Bass has explained. When a corpse has finished its service at the anthropology center, workers gather up its bones and give them a final cleaning. The bones are then added to the facility's skeleton collection, the largest collection of modern skeletons in the United States. Scientists have used this collection and others to create a data bank of bone measurements from almost 2,000 skeletons. Police and forensic anthropologists can consult this data bank by computer to determine the sex, race, age, and stature of unknown skeletons. Far from dishonoring the dead, Bass says, the Body Farm lets them reach beyond death to help others.

Chronology

1928	William M. Bass III born in Staunton, Virginia, on August 30
1951	Bass earns B.A. in psychology from University of Virginia
1951–53	Bass works at the Army Medical Research Laboratory in Fort Knox, Kentucky
1955	In April, Bass's physical anthropology professor at the University of Kentucky, Lexington, takes him on his first forensic anthropology case; later in the year, Bass changes his major from psychology to anthropology
1956	Bass earns master's degree in physical anthropology from University of Kentucky
1957–70	Bass spends summers in South Dakota excavating Arikara Indian burials as part of a Smithsonian Institution anthropology project

1961	Bass earns Ph.D. from University of Pennsylvania, Philadelphia
1961–71	Bass teaches physical anthropology at University of Kansas, Lawrence, and consults in forensic anthropology for Kansas Bureau of Investigation
1964	Cattle-rustling case makes Bass aware that little is known about what happens to bodies in the first weeks or months after death
1971	Bass moves to University of Tennessee, Knoxville, in June and becomes Tennessee's state forensic anthropologist
1972	Bass begins using deserted pig barn outside Knoxville to store corpses
1978	Bass examines a seemingly fresh corpse in a Civil War soldier's grave and misjudges the body's time of death by about 112 years
1980	Bass is given an acre (0.4 ha) of land behind the university medical school for a larger research facility; he and his students begin clearing the land in the fall
1981	Bass's facility receives its first donated body in May
1980s	Early in the decade, Bass's facility is given the name of Anthropological Research Facility (ARF); police and FBI agents begin calling it the Body Farm
1982–83	Bill Rodriguez, one of Bass's students, determines the succession of insect species that visit a corpse, helping to found forensic entomology; his research is published in fall 1983
1985	Academy of Forensic Sciences gives Bass an award; Council for Advancement and Support of Education chooses him as its National Professor of the Year
1990s	Early in the decade, Arpad Vass documents chemical changes that occur over time in soil beneath a body
	Late in the decade, ARF researchers develop a technique for using weather to help in determining time of death

1994	Patricia Cornwell publishes *The Body Farm*, a best-selling mystery novel that features a fictional version of ARF and brings publicity to the real facility
	In fall, a television station airs a program stating that ARF shows disrespect to veterans by using unclaimed bodies, some of which belonged to veterans; a bill is introduced into the Kentucky legislature to prevent ARF from accepting unclaimed bodies, but the measure is never passed
	Bass retires from teaching
1998	Bass retires from directorship of ARF
1999	ARF expands and changes its name to Forensic Anthropology Center in June
2000s	Center scientists do research on "electronic nose" and use of ground-penetrating radar to detect buried bodies
	Center adds to collection of modern skeletons; develops data bank of bone measurements and computer program that allows police and forensic anthropologists to use the data bank to determine sex, race, age, and stature of unknown skeletons

Further Reading

Books

Bass, Bill, and Jon Jefferson. *Death's Acre: Inside the Legendary Forensic Lab, the Body Farm, Where the Dead Do Tell Tales.* New York: Putnam, 2003.
> Bass's autobiography and account of the development of the University of Tennessee's Anthropological Research Facility, commonly known as the Body Farm. The book includes descriptions of many cases in which determining the time of death proved vital in identifying criminals.

Cornwell, Patricia. *The Body Farm.* New York: Scribner, 1994.
> Mystery novel in which a fictionalized version of the Body Farm and William Bass play key roles.

Articles

"Corpses Find New Life in Forensic Research at Tennessee's Body Farm." *Dallas Morning News,* October 31, 2003: n.p.
Lists recent research projects at the University of Tennessee's Forensic Anthropology Center in Knoxville.

Gannon, Robert. "The Body Farm." *Popular Science* 251 (September 1997): 77–81.
Recounts research on forensic entomology (the study of insects feeding on corpses) at the University of Tennessee's Anthropological Research Facility and at Pennsylvania State University.

Pederson, Daniel. "Down on the Body Farm." *Newsweek* (October 23, 2000): 50 ff.
Briefly describes the Forensic Anthropology Center at the University of Tennessee, Knoxville, popularly known as the Body Farm.

Ramsland, Katherine. "The Body Farm." Available online. URL: http://www.crimelibrary.com/criminal_mind/forensics/bill_bass. Accessed on September 25, 2005.
Series of articles, part of the Court TV crime library, that describes the work of William Bass at the Forensic Anthropology Center.

Rodriguez, W. C., and W. M. Bass. "Insect Activity and Its Relationship to Decay Rates of Human Cadavers in East Tennessee." *Journal of Forensic Sciences* 28 (1983): 423–432.
Scientific paper describing the order in which insects invade human corpses and how this succession can be used to determine how long ago a body died.

10

THE ULTIMATE IDENTIFIER

ALEC JEFFREYS AND DNA PROFILING

Forensic scientists can examine blood, bones, voices, and finger-prints to identify criminals and their victims. Still, even with fin-gerprints, the most dependable of these sources of identity, scientists disagree about how surely one person can be distinguished from all others. Determining identity without question seemed impossible until 1984, when British researcher Alec Jeffreys found an identity test that depends on the very material that defines an individual body: DNA, the substance of which genes are made.

Scientists showed in the early 1950s that DNA (deoxyribonucleic acid) carries information inherited from parents that controls a body's shape and function. The information is coded into the order, or sequence, in which four types of small molecules called bases are arranged along the double "backbone" of the larger DNA molecule. The DNA molecule has a shape termed a *double helix,* which looks like a twisted ladder. Almost every cell in a human, plant, or animal contains a complete, identical copy of that individual's DNA.

Researchers worked out the basic pattern of the genetic code by 1967. They then set out to identify individual genes—units of DNA that tell a cell how to make particular proteins, the large family of chemicals that does most of the work in cells. Alec Jeffreys was one of many researchers who took on this task. The surprising result of one of his experiments turned his work in a direction that greatly enriched forensic science.

The surprising result of a genetics experiment in September 1984 led Professor Sir Alec Jeffreys of the University of Leicester in Britain to invent the test that has come to be known as DNA profiling. (Anita Corbin, John O'Grady, and the British Council)

Presents Spark a Career

Alec John Jeffreys traces his interest in science to two presents that his parents, Sidney Victor and Joan (Knight) Jeffreys, gave him when he was a child: a microscope and a chemistry set. Thanks to these gifts, Jeffreys, born on January 9, 1950, in Oxford, England, became fascinated with biology, chemistry, and the interactions between the two. Not surprisingly, when he attended Merton College, part of Oxford University, he majored in biochemistry, the study of chemical reactions in the bodies of living things. He earned a B.A. in biochemistry in 1972 and a Ph.D. in 1975. During his

THE STRUCTURE OF DNA

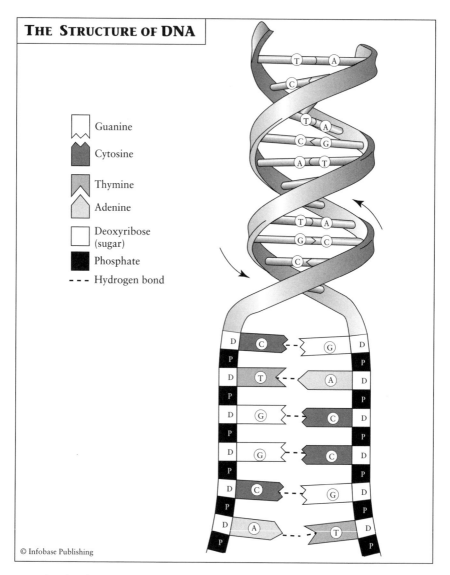

Guanine

Cytosine

Thymine

Adenine

Deoxyribose (sugar)

Phosphate

- - - Hydrogen bond

© Infobase Publishing

A molecule of DNA (deoxyribonucleic acid) is made up of two strands of material twined around each other in a shape like a twisted ladder, called a double helix. The sides of the ladder are made of alternating smaller molecules of phosphate (P) and deoxyribose (D), a sugar. The ladder's rungs are pairs of four kinds of bases, connected by hydrogen bonds. Adenine (A) always pairs with thymine (T), and cytosine (C) always pairs with guanine (G). The inherited information carried by a DNA molecule is coded into the order, or sequence, of bases in the molecule.

Oxford years, Jeffreys also became interested in genetics, the study of inherited information.

Jeffreys worked at the University of Amsterdam from 1975 to 1977 with another British scientist, Richard Flavell, developing methods for identifying individual genes. Jeffreys then returned to England and joined the department of genetics at the University of Leicester, where he still works. He became a full professor of genetics there in 1987.

At Leicester, Jeffreys studied how the sequence of bases in DNA differs from one human being to another. The variations are slight, amounting to only 0.1 percent of the total number of bases. Some of the differences occur in segments called hypervariable regions, which are made up of short sequences of bases repeated many times—a sort of genetic stutter. Different people can show dramatic differences in the number of repetitions, but within a family, the number of variations is usually passed on from parent to child.

Hypervariable regions are scattered throughout the human genome, or collection of genes. Most of these segments have no known function. Jeffreys and other geneticists nonetheless thought that the regions might be extremely useful as markers to help in locating other genetic differences that cause inherited diseases. Jeffreys therefore set out to develop a test that would let him detect hypervariable regions wherever they appeared.

A "Eureka!" Moment

Alec Jeffreys was not thinking about forensic science when he came into his office on the morning of September 10, 1984. He simply wanted to see how well his new test for hypervariable regions was working.

In 1983, Jeffreys had discovered a sequence of bases that many hypervariable regions seemed to share. Hoping to use this segment as a probe to "fish out" other hypervariable regions in DNA, he made copies of the sequence and added radioactive atoms to them. He expected the radioactive sequences to attach themselves to similar sequences in the DNA being tested. He also adapted a technique invented by Edwin Southern, another British scientist, to break up the test DNA into many fragments, arrange them by size on a membrane, and detect the hypervariable fragments by means of the radioactive sequence. If his test worked properly, the radioactivity from the atoms in his artificial sequences would darken an X-ray film. Any DNA fragments containing the radioactive sequences would appear as black bands on the resulting photograph.

Jeffreys had added his radioactive sequences to DNA from several human beings as well as different types of animals, exposed X-ray film to the DNA, and left the film to develop over the weekend. When he took his photograph out of the developing solution on that September morning, he expected to see just a few random lines. Instead, he discovered a definite pattern, much like the bar codes that identify items to computers in supermarket cash registers. "I took one look, thought 'what a complicated mess,' then suddenly realized we had patterns," Jeffreys stated in a Wellcome Trust article about his invention of DNA profiling. "It was a 'eureka!' moment. Standing in front of this picture in the darkroom, my life took a complete turn."

Jeffreys called his coworkers to look at the astonishing X-ray picture. The group realized almost immediately that Jeffreys had found a way to use DNA to distinguish one person from another. They confirmed this by pricking their fingers and testing samples of their blood. Each sample showed a different pattern of light and dark bars.

Reuniting a Family

By the afternoon of that thrilling day, Jeffreys had decided to call his technique "DNA fingerprinting." He and the other scientists discussed possible uses for the new test. The most obvious application was in paternity suits, civil suits in which a woman claims that a man is the father of her child but the man denies it. DNA is inherited, so parents and children would be expected to show similar DNA patterns in Jeffreys's test. Jeffreys's wife, the former Susan Miles, pointed out that the test might also settle immigration disputes, which often hinged on family relationships. The group thought that the technology could identify criminals and victims of crimes as well.

Jeffreys improved his test during the next several months and published two articles about it in *Nature* in 1985. Realizing that the technology was potentially valuable, he also patented it.

DNA testing was put to its first forensic use in an immigration case in March 1985. The case centered on a boy born in Ghana, a former British colony in West Africa, who had gone to Africa to visit his father. When the boy returned to Britain, where his mother and brothers and sisters lived, British immigration authorities claimed that he had forged his passport and threatened to deport him.

In order to stay with his family, who were British citizens, the boy had to prove that he was biologically related to them. A lawyer assisting the family read a newspaper article about Jeffreys's new technique and asked the scientist to test the boy's blood. The boy's mother and three siblings provided samples of their blood for comparison. The test showed that the boy was unquestionably closely related to the mother and the other children, so the immigration officials withdrew their accusations. This success, which Jeffreys (in a second Wellcome Trust article) called "a good news story of 'science fighting bureaucracy and helping families,'" received wide publicity.

Freeing an Innocent Man

Detectives quickly realized that Jeffreys's test could be a godsend for forensic science. Criminals or unidentified victims often leave blood, saliva, or other bodily fluids at crime scenes. These fluids usually include cells, which in turn contain DNA. Comparing DNA in such fluids with samples from suspects or victims' family members could provide valuable clues to identity.

The first murder case in which DNA testing was used began in November 1983, when Lynda Mann, a teenage girl, was found raped and strangled in Enderby, England. Three years later, in July 1986, the body of a second teenager, Dawn Ashworth, was discovered nearby. She appeared to have been attacked by the same person who had killed Mann.

Questioning suspects, police quickly focused on a young man who worked at a local mental hospital. After repeated interviews, the

CONNECTIONS: THE INNOCENCE PROJECT

Alec Jeffreys has said he is proud of the fact that DNA profiling's first forensic use was to demonstrate a suspect's innocence. Attorneys quickly realized that DNA evidence might free other people who insisted that they had committed no crimes, even though they had already been convicted and sent to prison.

In 1992, acting on this idea, New York attorneys Barry C. Scheck and Peter J. Neufeld established what they called the Innocence Project. The project, a nonprofit legal clinic, is part of the Benjamin N. Cardozo School of Law at Yeshiva University. It handles only cases in which postconviction DNA testing can potentially yield conclusive proof of a person's innocence.

As of August 2006, the Innocence Project had cleared 183 people of murder, rape, and other serious crimes. Some of these people had been in prison for more than 10 years before testing proved that they could not have committed the offenses for which they had been jailed. Some had been on Death Row. "Most of our clients are poor, forgotten, and have used up all of their legal avenues for relief," the project's Web site states.

Some convicts have even claimed a constitutional right to forensic DNA testing. One was James Harvey, convicted of rape and related crimes in Virginia in 1990. His DNA was compared with DNA in semen from the rape victim at the time of his trial, but DNA testing in those days was crude, and the results were unclear. In 1993, with the help of the Innocence Project, Harvey's attorneys asked for access to the rape kit containing the semen so that the test could be repeated with better technology. A federal district judge in Virginia ruled in July 2000 that the lawyers should have access to the kit. The Fourth U.S. Circuit Court of Appeals reversed the judge's decision in January 2002, but Harvey's attorneys obtained the kit a month later under a new state law. Ironically, when the DNA test was finally performed, it confirmed that Harvey was guilty.

man admitted that he had met Dawn Ashworth and said he might have killed her. He claimed not to remember the crime, however, and he insisted that he knew nothing about Lynda Mann's murder.

The villages in which the crimes had occurred were only about 10 miles (16 km) from the University of Leicester. A detective investigating the case had read about Jeffreys's test, and he took semen from the two girls' bodies and a sample of the young man's blood to the Leicester scientist and asked him to compare their DNA. After doing so, Jeffreys reported that the two semen samples matched each other, confirming that both girls had been attacked by the same killer. Neither matched the sample from the suspect, however. In spite of his confession, the mental hospital worker could not have committed the crimes, Jeffreys said. Taking Jeffreys at his word, the police released the young man in November. "The first time DNA profiling was used in criminology, it was to prove innocence," Jeffreys pointed out in a Wellcome Trust article.

Dragnet of Blood

More determined than ever to find the killer of Lynda Mann and Dawn Ashworth, David Baker, chief superintendent of the Leicestershire police, decided on a bold move. He would ask every man between the ages of 17 and 34 who lived in the three villages near the crime scenes—about 4,500 men—to donate a sample of blood for DNA testing. Police could not force anyone to give blood, but they believed that social pressure would make most men cooperate.

The testing began in January 1987. Ninety percent of the samples were ruled out quickly because they showed a blood type different from that of the man who had left the semen. Testing the remaining 10 percent required many months because each test took days or even weeks.

All the men in the villages seemed to have provided donations, but Home Office forensic scientists using Jeffreys's techniques found that none of the samples matched the ones from the crime scenes. Baker had no idea how to proceed until August, when a woman reported a conversation she had heard in a local pub, or bar. She and several other people who worked for a nearby bakery had gone to the pub for lunch, and one of the bakery workers, Ian Kelly, told his friends that he had fooled the police by giving a blood sample under the name of another employee, Colin Pitchfork. Pitchfork had a

(Opposite page) *In the classic form of Alec Jeffreys's DNA profiling test, DNA is recovered from the nuclei of cells taken from a biological fluid such as blood or semen. Enzymes (a type of protein) from bacteria break the DNA into fragments. The fragments are separated according to size by a process called gel electrophoresis and placed on a membrane. The tester then adds radioactive segments of DNA, which will attach themselves to sequences in the test DNA that vary from person to person. The membrane, which contains DNA samples from the crime scene, suspect, and victim on different "tracks," is then exposed to X-ray film. When the film is developed, it reveals patterns that look like supermarket bar codes. A computer can compare the patterns to determine whether the crime scene sample came from a suspect, a victim, or someone else.*

minor criminal record, Kelly said, and he had told Kelly that he was afraid the police would harass him if he provided his own sample. He begged Kelly to take his place, and, using a forged passport, Kelly had done so.

Police immediately questioned Kelly, who repeated his story. They then visited Pitchfork. Pitchfork confessed to both murders almost immediately. Not wanting to risk another mistaken arrest, Baker gave forensic scientists some of Pitchfork's blood. They tested the blood and reported that Pitchfork's DNA matched the DNA in the semen samples. Pitchfork pleaded guilty to both murders in January 1988 and was given two sentences of life in prison.

Improving the Test

DNA profiling's contribution to Colin Pitchfork's capture made headlines around the world. Police and prosecutors hailed the new test as almost a miracle, and other countries quickly adopted it. In early 1988, for example, Tommy Lee Andrews, a warehouse worker in Orlando, Florida, was convicted of two rapes partly on the basis of DNA evidence. Andrews was the first person in the United States to be "fingered" for a major crime by his genes.

Alec Jeffreys's original DNA test had some drawbacks. Besides taking days to perform, it required large amounts of clean samples, which often were not available at crime scenes. It also could not be automated. Technological advances in the late 1980s and early 1990s improved the test, however.

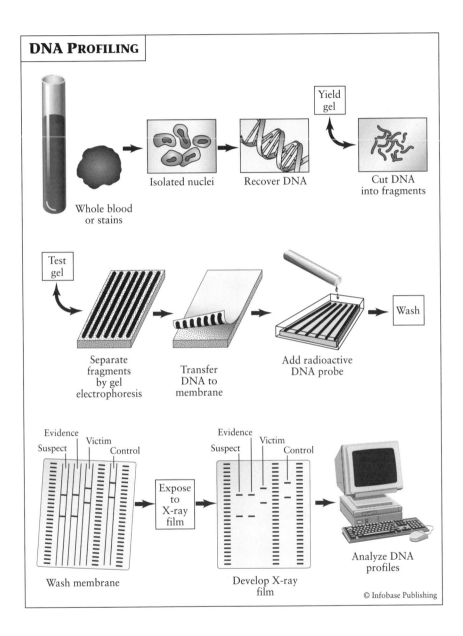

DNA PROFILING

Whole blood or stains

Isolated nuclei

Recover DNA

Yield gel

Cut DNA into fragments

Test gel

Separate fragments by gel electrophoresis

Transfer DNA to membrane

Add radioactive DNA probe

Wash

Evidence Suspect Victim Control

Wash membrane

Expose to X-ray film

Evidence Suspect Victim Control

Develop X-ray film

Analyze DNA profiles

© Infobase Publishing

The most important advance was the polymerase chain reaction, or PCR. First developed by U.S. scientist Kary Mullis in 1983, this reaction can duplicate a tiny sample of DNA, such as the amount

POLYMERASE CHAIN REACTION

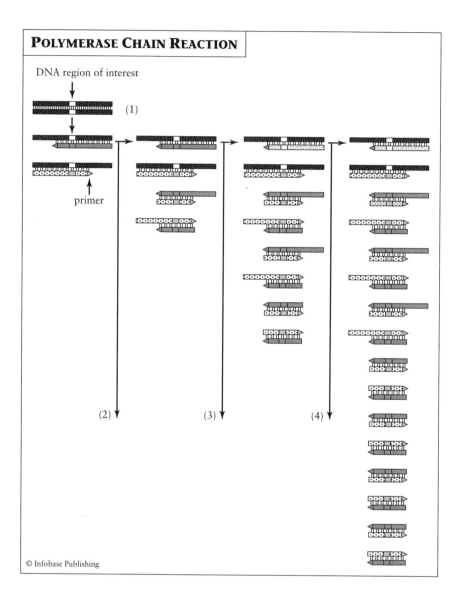

DNA region of interest

(1)

primer

(2)　　　　(3)　　　　(4)

© Infobase Publishing

found in the tiniest droplet of blood or semen, a million times in a few hours. This duplication creates an amount of DNA large enough to test. Jeffreys's test was combined with PCR in 1989 to produce a new procedure that was far more sensitive, cheaper,

(Opposite page) *The polymerase chain reaction, first developed in 1983, provides a fast way to produce huge numbers of copies of a segment of DNA. First, the sample of DNA intended for duplication is heated to separate the two strands of the molecule. Primer containing the smaller molecules that make up a DNA molecule is added, along with an enzyme that can join the smaller molecules together to make a duplicate strand that attaches to each of the single strands of the test molecule. The result is two identical, double-stranded segments where only one segment had existed before. The process is rapidly repeated, over and over, doubling the number of identical segments each time. PCR can be applied to tiny amounts of DNA, such as the quantity found in a small drop of blood, to create samples large enough to be tested by DNA profiling.*

faster, and easier to read than the original test. The new test could also be computerized.

A second improvement, made by Jeffreys and his team in 1990, redesigned the test to search for shorter stretches of repeating DNA than the ones he had used at first. The modern version of DNA profiling looks for these segments, termed short tandem repeats (STRs), at several places within a DNA molecule. Automated profiling kits used in Britain test 10 different segments, while those used in the United States test 13 segments.

In the years since a few drops of blood proved Colin Pitchfork's guilt, DNA profiling has solved all kinds of forensic cases. In 1990, for example, Alec Jeffreys compared DNA from the wife and son of Nazi mass killer Josef Mengele to DNA from the bones that forensic anthropologist Clyde Snow and other experts had examined in Brazil in 1985 and declared to be those of Mengele. Jeffreys reported that certain features of the DNA in the Brazilian skeleton were very similar to those in the

Today machines can carry out a combination of PCR and DNA profiling automatically, producing results in just a few hours. (FBI)

OTHER SCIENTISTS: MARY-CLAIRE KING (1946–)

Even before Alec Jeffreys used DNA profiling to confirm Clyde Snow's identification of Josef Mengele's skeleton, geneticist Mary-Claire King applied a different DNA test to help some of the same survivors of the "disappeared" in Argentina that Snow's exhumation of bones in mass graves was aiding. King's test helped relatives find some of the children that people killed by the Argentine military government had left behind.

King was born in Wilmette, Illinois, on February 27, 1946. A childhood love of puzzles drew her to mathematics, which became her major at Carleton College in Minnesota. After graduating from Carleton, she studied genetics at the University of California, Berkeley, earning a Ph.D. in 1973 with research showing that humans share more than 99 percent of their DNA with chimpanzees.

King's work in Argentina began in 1984, about the same time that Clyde Snow was starting to unearth the bones of the disappeared and Alec Jeffreys was discovering his "bar code" DNA X-ray photo. A group called the Abuelas de Plaza de Mayo (Grandmothers of the Plaza of May), made up of relatives of the disappeared, asked King, then on the faculty of the Berkeley campus, to help them identify their grandchildren. The children, captured with their parents or born in prison, had been sold or given away, and many of the families who acquired them refused to give them up unless the grandmothers could prove their kinship.

To demonstrate the relationship, King did not use the DNA in the nucleus (central body) of cells, which was the form that Jeffreys and most other geneticists studied. Instead, she turned to the DNA in mitochondria, tiny bodies that help cells use energy. DNA in the nucleus is inherited from both parents, but the DNA in mitochondria comes only from the mother. It therefore is especially useful in showing the relationship between a child and female relatives. King's tests of mitochondrial DNA reunited more than 50 Argentinean children with their birth families.

DNA of Mengele's son. His test finally convinced even the suspicious Israeli government that the man who had died in Brazil really was Mengele.

DNA Databases

As had happened with other new forensic technologies, experts argued in court about the value of DNA profiling during the early 1990s. By the middle of the decade, however, evidence from DNA testing was widely accepted. Questions of contamination or poor testing procedures were raised in some trials, such as the famous murder trial of African-American football star O. J. Simpson in 1995. Experts generally agreed, however, that when DNA tests were performed by properly trained people on clean samples, the results were extremely reliable. The chance that two unrelated people will have the same patterns at all 13 of the spots examined in a modern DNA profile is said to be less than one in 100 billion—perhaps as low as one in a quadrillion.

As DNA testing became widespread, police realized that DNA "bar codes," like fingerprints, could be stored in computerized databases for use in future identification of criminals. In April 1995, Britain began assembling a database of DNA samples from all people convicted of crimes serious enough to earn prison sentences. Germany, France, South Africa, Canada, China, Australia, and many other countries later set up similar databases. All 50 states in the United States have authorized establishment of databases containing DNA profiles from criminals, and the FBI set up a federal database, the National DNA Index System (NDIS), in 1998. The bureau also manages the Combined DNA Index System (CODIS), computer software that coordinates national, state, and local databases so that police can match samples from crime scenes with DNA profiles of convicted felons anywhere in the country.

The Jewel in the Crown

Alec Jeffreys has received many honors for his invention of "DNA fingerprinting" and other contributions to genetics. He was knighted in 1994, for example. The Royal Society, Britain's most highly regarded scientific organization, gave Jeffreys its Davy Medal in 1987, made him Wolfson Research Professor in 1991, and awarded him a Royal Medal in 2004. Jeffreys won the Australia Prize in 1998

SOCIAL IMPACT: BOON TO DETECTIVES OR THREAT TO PRIVACY?

DNA databases, like fingerprint databases, have proved extremely useful in helping police track criminals who move from place to place. They have also allowed detectives to close "cold cases"—crimes that had remained unsolved for many years. Some police officials and prosecutors therefore have urged that the databases be expanded to include profiles from all people charged with a crime or even perhaps investigated in connection with a crime, whether or not the people were convicted of any wrongdoing. Britain established such an expanded database in 2003.

Civil rights advocates such as the American Civil Liberties Union say that expanded DNA databases would invade the privacy of people who are not criminals. Especially if DNA samples themselves are kept, rather than just profiles (which do not reflect functioning genes), these critics fear that personal information such as medical history or racial ancestry could be deduced from the databases. They also believe that police or others might discriminate against people who appear in a DNA database.

Alec Jeffreys himself is concerned about possible abuses of expanded DNA databases. Jeffreys's solution is not restricting the databases, however. Instead, he thinks that all citizens' DNA profiles should be recorded. "If we're all on the database, no one is being discriminated against," Jeffreys stated in a Wellcome Trust article. Jeffreys believes that only profiles should be kept and that the database should be managed by the government agency that records births and deaths, not by the police.

---

and the Louis-Jeantet Prize for Medicine, a major European award for biomedical research, in 2004. He was inducted into the U.S. National Inventors Hall of Fame in May 2005 and won the prestigious Lasker Award from the Albert and Mary Lasker Foundation in September.

Leaving the refinement of DNA profiling to others, Jeffreys has focused his own research on basic genetics. Most of his work has concerned mutations, or changes in genes. In 1996, for instance, he and Yuri Dubrova of the University of Moscow reported that DNA profiles of children born to people exposed to radiation from the meltdown of a nuclear power-plant reactor in Chernobyl, Ukraine, in 1986 showed twice as many mutations as profiles of children from English families. Jeffreys and Dubrova's work provided the first evidence that radiation could produce inheritable mutations in humans. Jeffreys is trying to discover the genetic mechanism that triggers these mutations. He also hopes to learn more about mutations that cause disease.

Important as this work may be, Jeffreys feels that the development of "DNA fingerprinting" has been his greatest scientific contribution. "It totally revolutionized forensic science," he said in a 1997 interview published in *Chemistry and Industry*. An article in the August 11, 2000, issue of the highly respected journal *Science* agreed, calling DNA profiling "the jewel in the crown of modern forensics."

Chronology

1950	Alec John Jeffreys born in Oxford, England, on January 9
1950s	Early in the decade, scientists in Britain and the United States show that DNA (deoxyribonucleic acid) carries inherited information that controls a body's shape and function and that the information is coded into the sequence of bases in the DNA molecule
1967	Scientists finish translating the genetic code
1972	Jeffreys earns B.A. in biochemistry from Merton College, Oxford University
1975	Jeffreys earns D.Phil. (Ph.D.) from Merton College
1975–77	Jeffreys works at University of Amsterdam with Richard Flavell
1977	Jeffreys joins faculty of University of Leicester (England)
1983	Jeffreys discovers a sequence of bases that hypervariable regions of DNA seem to share
	Lynda Mann is raped and strangled in Enderby, England

	Kary Mullis discovers the polymerase chain reaction (PCR), which rapidly reproduces fragments of DNA
1984	Jeffreys begins developing a test that will use his sequence to identify hypervariable regions wherever they appear in DNA; on the morning of September 10, he produces an X-ray photograph that shows individual variations in DNA; he and his coworkers discuss uses for what he terms *DNA fingerprinting*
	Mary-Claire King begins using tests of DNA in mitochondria to identify children removed from their homes by the former military government in Argentina
1985	In March, Jeffreys's DNA test is used to resolve an immigration dispute
	Jeffreys publishes two articles about his test in *Nature* and patents the test
1986	In July, Dawn Ashworth is killed in the same manner as Lynda Mann; police question a young man who confesses to killing Ashworth; Jeffreys compares the man's DNA to semen collected from Ashworth and Mann and concludes that the accused man could not have committed either crime; the man is released in November
1987	Beginning in January, police collect blood samples from about 4,500 men living in the area where Mann and Ashworth were killed; in August, a report that a man submitted a sample under the name of another leads to questioning of the second man, Colin Pitchfork; Pitchfork confesses to the murders; his DNA is shown to match that in the semen samples
	Jeffreys becomes full professor of genetics at University of Leicester
1988	Pitchfork pleads guilty to the murders of Mann and Ashworth in January, becoming the first person convicted of murder partly through DNA evidence
	Early in the year, Tommy Lee Andrews becomes the first person in the United States to be convicted of a major crime (rape) partly through DNA evidence
1989	Jeffreys's test is combined with PCR, a major improvement

1990	Jeffreys's group begins to perform DNA profiling with short tandem repeats; Jeffreys uses this form of profiling to confirm that bones unearthed in Brazil in 1985 belonged to Nazi war criminal Josef Mengele
1992	New York attorneys Barry C. Scheck and Peter J. Neufeld establish the Innocence Project, which uses DNA testing to demonstrate innocence of some convicted criminals
1994	Jeffreys is knighted
1995	In April, Britain establishes world's first database containing DNA of convicted criminals
	Questions about possible contamination of DNA evidence leads to acquittal in murder trial of football star O. J. Simpson in October
1996	Jeffreys and Yuri Dubrova report that DNA profiles of children from families exposed to radiation from the Chernobyl (Ukraine) nuclear power-plant meltdown show twice as many mutations as those of children not exposed to radiation
1998	FBI establishes National DNA Index System, a national database of DNA profiles of convicted criminals
	Jeffreys wins Australia Prize
2003	Britain expands its DNA database to include all people tested in connection with crimes, whether or not they were convicted of wrongdoing
2004	Jeffreys wins Royal Medal from Royal Society and Louis-Jeantet Prize for Medicine
2005	Jeffreys is inducted into U.S. National Inventors Hall of Fame in May and wins Lasker Award in September

Further Reading

Books

Fridell, Ron. *Solving Crimes: Pioneers of Forensic Science.* New York: Franklin Watts, 2000.

Contains a chapter on Alec Jeffreys and the use of DNA profiling in forensics.

Genge, N. E. *The Forensic Casebook.* New York: Ballantine Books, 2002.
Includes description of modern forensic DNA testing.

Wilson, Colin, and Damon Wilson. *Written in Blood: A History of Forensic Detection.* New York: Carroll & Graf reissue, 2003.
Contains material on the Colin Pitchfork case and other early criminal cases in which DNA testing was used.

Yeatts, Tabatha. *Forensics: Solving the Crime.* Minneapolis: Oliver Press, 2001.
Contains a chapter on Jeffreys and the discovery of DNA fingerprinting.

Yount, Lisa. *Biotechnology and Genetic Engineering.* Rev. ed. New York: Facts On File, 2004.
Includes material on forensic DNA testing and DNA databases, as well as descriptions of key court cases in which DNA profiling played a part.

Articles

"Alec John Jeffreys." In *Notable Scientists: From 1900 to the Present.* Farmington Hills, Mich: Gale Group, 2001.
Brief account of Jeffreys's life and career, including recent honors he has received.

Amirani, Amir. "Sir Alec Jeffreys on DNA Profiling and Minisatellites." ScienceWatch. Available online. URL: http://www.sciencewatch.com/interviews/sir_alec_jeffreys.htm. Posted in 1995. Accessed on September 24, 2005.
Interview with Jeffreys and summary of his career, focusing on his research in basic genetics.

Chapman, Tim. "From Antarctica to Chernobyl." *Chemistry and Industry,* November 17, 1997, pp. 899–900.
Lists Jeffreys's research achievements, including detection of high rates of genetic mutation in children exposed to radiation from the meltdown of a nuclear power plant in Chernobyl, Ukraine, in 1986.

Dubrova, Y. E., et al. "Human Minisatellite Mutation Rate after the Chernobyl Accident." *Nature* 380 (1996): 683–686.

Scientific paper describing an increased rate of mutation (genetic change) in children born to parents exposed to radiation from the nuclear power-plant meltdown in Chernobyl. Alec Jeffreys contributed to the research.

Jeffreys, A. J., V. Wilson, and S. L. Thein. "Hypervariable 'minisatellite' regions in human DNA." *Nature* 314 (1985): 67–73.

Scientific paper describing the Jeffreys laboratory's development of a test that revealed highly variable regions of human DNA and could be used to show individual differences in DNA.

———. "Individual-specific Fingerprints of Human DNA." *Nature* 316 (1985): 76–79.

Further develops the idea of "DNA fingerprinting."

Strutt, Michael. "Legally Scientific?" Justice Action. Available online. URL: http://home.iprimus.com.au/dna_info/dna/JA_DNA_LegSci_1.html. Accessed on September 24, 2005.

Lengthy criticism of the validity of forensic DNA testing.

Web Site

The Wellcome Trust. "Genes and the Body: Human Variation." URL: http://genome.wellcome.ac.uk/en/genome/node30030.html. Posted on December 2, 2004. Accessed on September 24, 2005.

Includes articles that describe the discovery of DNA "fingerprinting," the first uses of the new technology, and the debate about DNA identification databases.

CHRONOLOGY

700	Chinese use fingerprints to establish identity on documents
1200	Handguns invented in Middle East
1490s	Gunsmiths begin adding rifling (spiral grooves) inside gun barrels to make bullets spin
1813	Mathieu-Joseph-Bonaventure Orfila writes *Traité des poisons*, the first toxicology text
1836	James Marsh invents reliable test for arsenic
1840	Mathieu Orfila serves as expert witness in Lafarge poisoning case in France
1841	Edgar Allan Poe writes "Murders in the Rue Morgue," first fictional detective story
1858	William Herschel first uses palm print as identification on a contract in India
1880	Henry Faulds writes letter to *Nature* describing use of fingerprints for identification and solving crimes
1880s	Alphonse Bertillon establishes anthropometry as method of identifying repeat criminals
1885	Cesare Lombroso measures blood pressure of crime suspects during police interviews to determine whether they are lying
1887	Arthur Conan Doyle publishes first Sherlock Holmes story, "A Study in Scarlet"

1889	Alexandre Lacassagne solves a crime by using a microscope to compare markings on bullet from crime scene to those on bullet test-fired from suspect's gun; identifies a badly decomposed body by examining its bones
1890s	European scientists develop tables for determining stature from measurement of long bones and for showing thickness of skin and muscle in various parts of the face Late in the decade, Edward Henry and associates in India develop practical fingerprint classification system
1892	Francis Galton publishes *Finger Prints*
1893	Hans Gross publishes *Criminal Investigation*
1900–01	Karl Landsteiner describes blood types
1901	Henry establishes fingerprint bureau within detective branch of London metropolitan police (Scotland Yard) Paul Uhlenhuth develops test to distinguish between human and animal blood and applies it in a murder case
1902	Karl Landsteiner and Max Richter recommend typing blood in bloodstains from crime scenes as a way of solving crimes
1905	Stratton brothers convicted of murder in first British murder case using fingerprint evidence in court
1910	Edmond Locard establishes world's first forensic science laboratory in Lyon, France
1912	Locard solves murder case by identifying trace evidence; writes *Treatise on Criminalistics* Hans Gross founds first criminological institute at University of Graz, Austria
1915	Leon Lattes in Turin, Italy, develops improved method for identifying blood types in dried bloodstains and begins using blood typing regularly to solve crimes
1919–23	Charles Waite creates database of rifling of guns made in United States and Europe

1921	John Larson develops first polygraph in Berkeley, California
1923	Appeals court decision in *Frye v. United States* states that a technology must be accepted by the scientific community before results of tests using that technology can be admitted as evidence in court
	Charles Waite annd others establish Bureau of Forensic Ballistics in New York City
1926	Leonarde Keeler adds tool for measuring galvanic skin response to Larson's polygraph
1927	In an appeal of the Sacco-Vanzetti murder case, Calvin Goddard concludes that the bullets that killed a guard during a robbery came from Sacco's gun
1929–30	Goddard examines bullets and guns from St. Valentine's Day Massacre; he establishes Scientific Crime Detection Laboratory at Northwestern University, near Chicago
1930s	Keeler popularizes the polygraph
1932	Federal Bureau of Investigation (FBI) establishes crime laboratory
1941	Lawrence G. Kersta and other engineers at Bell Telephone Laboratories create sound spectrograph (automatic sound analyzer) for possible military use during World War II
1940s, 1950s	U.S. scientists revise physical anthropology tables after studying remains of soldiers killed in World War II and Korean War
1960	Kersta creates improved sound spectrograph
1962	Kersta publishes article in *Nature* describing research on 50,000 voices and claiming that each voice produces unique recordings on sound spectrograph
1967	Sound spectrograph (voiceprint) evidence first used in a trial
1977	FBI establishes Automated Fingerprint Identification System (AFIS)

1979	Clyde Snow identifies remains of people killed in crash of American Airlines flight 191; he identifies remains of victims of serial killer John Wayne Gacy
1980	FBI creates General Rifling Characteristics file
	William M. Bass III establishes Anthropological Research Facility (ARF, later the Forensic Anthropology Center), popularly known as the Body Farm, at the University of Tennessee, Knoxville
1983	Research of Bill Rodriguez on insect succession at ARF helps to establish forensic entomology
	Kary Mullis develops polymerase chain reaction (PCR)
1984	Alec Jeffreys develops DNA identification (profiling) test
	Snow begins identifying remains of citizens killed by former military government in Argentina; Mary-Claire King begins comparing mitochondrial DNA to prove relationships between children of the "disappeared" in Argentina and their grandmothers
1985	Snow testifies in trial of nine leaders of former Argentine military government in April and helps to obtain murder convictions against five of them; in June, Snow and other forensic experts identify remains of a man who drowned in Brazil in 1979 as notorious Nazi war criminal Josef Mengele
1986	First use of DNA profiling to demonstrate innocence and guilt in a murder case
1988	U.S. Congress passes Employee Polygraph Protection Act, which prohibits most private employers (but not government agencies) from using polygraph tests for employee screening
	DNA profiling combined with PCR to produce faster, more accurate test
1989	FBI introduces Drugfire, database and automated comparison system for bullets, cartridges, and shell casings
1992	Barry Scheck and Peter Neufeld establish Innocence Project, which uses DNA testing in attempts to prove innocence of certain convicted criminals

1993	In *Daubert v. Merrell Dow Pharmaceuticals,* U.S. Supreme Court rules that individual judges should determine which scientific evidence to allow in court cases
1995	Britain establishes world's first database of DNA profiles of convicted criminals
	Accusations that DNA evidence was contaminatd help to produce acquittal in murder trial of African-American football star O. J. Simpson in October
1996	Clyde Snow and Argentine forensic anthropology team excavate mass grave near Vukovar, in the former Yugoslavia
1998	FBI establishes National DNA Index System (NDIS)
2003	Britain expands its DNA database to include all people tested in connection with crimes, whether or not they were convicted of wrongdoing

GLOSSARY

accumulated degree-days (ADD) formula developed by William Bass and others at the Forensic Anthropology Center (part of the University of Tennessee, Knoxville) that uses a combination of air temperature figures and the degree of a body's decomposition to determine how long ago a person died

alias a false name, especially one used for fraud or other criminal purposes

alkaloids a family of compounds found naturally in plants; many of its members, such as nicotine and atropine (belladonna), are poisonous

Anthropological Research Facility former name of facility at the University of Tennessee, Knoxville, now called the Forensic Anthropology Center; established in 1980 by William M. Bass III and his students, it conducts research on the decomposition of human corpses and is popularly known as the Body Farm

anthropology the study of primates (humans, apes, and monkeys), especially differences between them; subspecialties include physical anthropology and cultural anthropology. *See also* PHYSICAL ANTHROPOLOGY

anthropometry the technology of measuring parts of the body or physical traits such as strength; Alphonse Bertillon popularized its use for identification in the 1880s

antibody a protein in blood serum that attaches to a matching foreign protein (an antigen) and marks that protein and whatever carries it for destruction by the immune system; formerly called a precipitin. *See also* ANTIGEN

antigen a protein, usually found on the surfaces of cells, that can produce an immune response when recognized by an antibody. *See also* ANTIBODY; IMMUNE REACTION

181

arch a category of fingerprint in which the ridges do not turn. *Compare with* LOOP; WHORL

arsenic a metallic element (As) that is poisonous in most doses; in the form of white arsenic (arsenic oxide), it was commonly used as a murder weapon in some times and places

Arsenic Act a law passed in Britain in 1851 that required druggists to sell poisons, particularly arsenic, only to people whom they knew personally; individuals who bought poison also had to sign a "poison book" as a record of their purchases

arsenic mirror a test for arsenic developed by Johann Metzger in 1787; it depended on the fact that if a mixture containing arsenic was heated until it turned red, a layer of shiny black metallic arsenic would be deposited on any nearby cold surface, such as a plate

arsine a compound of arsenic and hydrogen, usually existing as a poisonous, garlicky-smelling gas

articulators the parts of the vocal system that form tones from the vocal cords into particular spoken sounds: the lips, teeth, tongue, soft palate, and jaw. *Compare with* RESONATORS

artifact any object made, modified, or used by humans

autopsy a medical examination of a dead body, usually done to determine the cause of death

bases four types of small molecules (adenine, cytosine, thymine, and guanine) found within the large DNA molecule; genetic information is encoded in the order, or sequence, of the bases in a DNA molecule. *See also* DNA; GENETIC CODE

biochemistry the study of chemical reactions in the bodies of living things

biometric identification identification through measurement or recording of unique physical features, such as fingerprints or markings in the iris (colored part) of the eye

blood bank a place where blood and blood products, refrigerated and treated with a preservative such as sodium citrate, are stored until needed; the first blood bank was developed by Bernard Fantus in 1937

blood type one of several groups into which humans can be divided, based on the type of antigens carried on the surface of their red blood cells; the most important blood types are A, B, O, and AB.

Blood types, also called blood groups, were discovered by Karl Landsteiner in 1900. *See also* ANTIGEN; RED BLOOD CELL

blowfly a species of shiny green fly that is usually the first insect to infest a body after death

Body Farm a popular nickname given to the Anthropological Research Facility (later the Forensic Anthropology Center) at the University of Tennessee, Knoxville

Bordet test a test developed by Paul Uhlenhuth in 1901 that permits samples of human blood to be distinguished from animal blood; also called the precipitin test

brain fingerprinting a technique developed by Iowa neuroscientist Lawrence A. Farwell that attempts to identify guilty knowledge by changes in brain waves that occur when a person views something familiar

caliber the diameter of the inside of a gun barrel, measured in inches

calipers an instrument with bent or curved legs, used to measure thickness

carrion beetle a type of beetle that arrives on a dead body after blowflies but before dermestid beetles; it feeds on both the body and blowfly larvae (maggots)

Caucasoid one of three main racial types; it refers to humans primarily from Europe, the Middle East (western Asia), North Africa, as well as parts of the Indian subcontinent and central Asia. *Compare with* MONGOLOID; NEGROID

chromatography any one of several techniques for separating substances in a mixture

circumstantial evidence indirect evidence, as opposed to eyewitness testimony; all physical evidence is circumstantial evidence

clotting a chemical reaction that causes blood to thicken when exposed to air

cold case a criminal case that has remained unsolved for a long period but remains open in the hope that it will eventually be solved

Combined DNA Index System (CODIS) computer software developed by the FBI that coordinates national, state, and local DNA profile databases in the United States. *See also* IAFS

comparison microscope a form of microscope that allows two objects, such as bullets, to be compared by viewing them side by side; it was developed by Philip O. Gravelle around 1923

control question a question asked as part of a polygraph examination that has nothing to do with the crime being investigated; it is not expected to produce a strong emotional reaction and is asked in order to obtain a recording of a person's baseline responses

coroner an appointed political official whose job includes determining the cause of suspicious deaths; he or she may or may not have medical experience. *Compare with* MEDICAL EXAMINER

cranium the top part of the skull, which encases the brain

criminalist sometimes, another term for forensic scientist; sometimes, another term for evidence technician, a person who gathers physical evidence at the scene of a crime

criminalistics the study of evidence, especially physical evidence, in criminal cases; sometimes used as a synonym for forensic science

criminology the study of criminals and criminal behavior

Daubert rule a ruling based on a U.S. Supreme Court decision in the case of *Daubert v. Merrell Dow Pharmaceuticals* in 1993; it states that individual judges should determine which scientific evidence to allow in court cases. *Compare with* FRYE STANDARD

dermestid beetle the last of several species of insects to arrive at a dead body and infest it; also called carpet beetle

detective someone who uses observation, logic, and technology to find hidden facts about a crime and identify the person or persons who committed it

DNA deoxyribonucleic acid, the complex molecules carrying the inherited information that controls a body's shape and function. *See also* BASES; GENE

DNA profiling a test, invented by Alec Jeffreys in 1984, in which certain regions in DNA that vary considerably from person to person are compared; the test can be used to determine identity because no two people except identical twins are thought to have the same DNA code in all the regions examined

Drugfire an electronic database containing hundreds of thousands of digital images of fired bullets and cartridge casings, developed by the FBI in 1989

eugenics the belief that the human race will be improved if individuals with desirable characteristics are encouraged to reproduce and those with undesirable traits are prevented from doing so

examining magistrate a legal official who combined some of the functions of a detective and a judge, investigating crimes and passing sentence on criminals

exchange principle a principle developed by Edmond Locard in the early 20th century, stating that everywhere a person contacts the environment, the person takes something away and leaves something behind

exhume to remove a buried body from its grave

facial reconstruction a process of using clay sculpture or, sometimes, computer graphics to produce an image of a deceased person's face, based on measurements of the person's skull

fingerprint a print of the curving lines on the fingertips, used for identification because no two people are thought to have exactly the same fingerprints. *See also* ARCH; HENRY SYSTEM; LOOP; WHORL

forensic anthropology the study and comparison of bodies after death, especially bones, in connection with crimes or other legal matters; a form of physical anthropology. *Compare with* FORENSIC PATHOLOGY

Forensic Anthropology Center name taken in 1999 by the former Anthropological Research Facility at the University of Tennessee, Knoxville (informally called the Body Farm); it is famous for its research on the decomposition of bodies after death, used by police to determine when a person died

forensic ballistics the study of guns, bullets, and bullet casings in connection with crimes or other legal matters; also called firearms identification

forensic entomology the study of insects in connection with crimes or other legal matters, usually focusing on insects that infest a body after death (which can be used to determine time of death)

forensic pathology the study of diseased or injured tissues (flesh), usually of a dead person, in connection with crimes or other legal matters. *Compare with* FORENSIC ANTHROPOLOGY

forensic science science applied to the investigation of crimes and other legal matters

frequency a measurement of how often the molecules of the air vibrate as sound waves pass them. Humans hear frequencies as pitch. *See also* PITCH

Frye **standard** a judicial ruling, made by an appeals court in 1923 in the case of *Frye v. United States,* stating that a science technique must be accepted by the scientific community in order for evidence or testimony based on that technique to be admitted in a court case. *Compare with* DAUBERT RULE

fundamentals the main sounds within a complex sound, such as a spoken tone. *See also* HARMONICS

galvanic skin response a measurement of how well the skin conducts electricity, which reflects the amount of sweat produced; an increase in sweat reflects stress, which may be associated with lying. Leonarde Keeler added a measurement of galvanic skin response to the polygraph in 1926.

gas chromatography a procedure for determining the chemical composition of a mixture in which the mixture is vaporized, or turned into gas, and then sent through a coiled glass tube; it is usually used together with mass spectrometry

gene a unit of DNA that tells a cell how to make a particular protein or performs some other specific function, such as controlling other genes

General Rifling Characteristics file a database, established by the FBI in 1980, that contains detailed measurements of the rifling in more than 18,000 types of guns

genetic code the order, or sequence, of bases within a DNA molecule that transmits inherited information

genetics the study of inherited information and its transmission from one generation to the next

genome an organism's complete collection of genes

grooves the depressed areas between raised areas (lands) in a gun barrel or on a bullet

guilty knowledge method a form of questioning used in polygraph tests, invented by University of Minnesota psychologist David Lykken in 1981, that focuses on people's reaction to knowledge about a crime that a person involved in it is expected to have

gunshot residue chemicals that spray out from a gun when the weapon is fired; these chemicals can be detected on the hands and clothing of a person who fired the gun, stood close by, or handled the weapon soon after firing

harmonics faint overtones in a complex sound such as a spoken word or music; they are multiples of the fundamentals in the sound. *Compare with* FUNDAMENTALS

helix the twist (either right or left) or corkscrew shape of the rifling in a gun barrel

helixometer a device, invented by John H. Fisher around 1923, used to look into a gun barrel and examine the twist, or helix, of the barrel's rifling; it consists of a long, hollow probe with an attached light and magnifying glass

hemoglobin the red, iron-containing pigment in blood that carries oxygen to the tissues of the body

Henry system a system of fingerprint classification developed by Edward Henry, Azizal (Azial) Haque, and Hemchandra Bose in India around 1897

hypervariable region a segment of DNA, with no known function and consisting of a series of short repeated sequences, that varies from person to person; Alec Jeffreys used comparison of these regions in the identification test (DNA profiling) that he developed in 1984

immune reaction a reaction in which cells and chemicals in the immune system detect and destroy proteins (antigens) foreign to the body

immune system the body's defense system, consisting of cells and chemicals (proteins) in the blood and certain other body fluids

immunity resistance to diseases caused by microorganisms, produced by the immune system (sometimes with outside stimulation in the form of vaccines)

impressed prints fingerprints appearing as three-dimensional marks pressed into clay, soap, or other soft surfaces; also called plastic prints. *Compare with* LATENT PRINTS; PATENT PRINTS

"inheritance powder" a nickname for white arsenic (arsenic oxide), given because that substance was often used in 17th-century France to poison rich relatives

Integrated Automatic Fingerprint Identification System (IAFIS) a national electronic database of fingerprints of convicted criminals, developed by the FBI in 1999. *See also* CODIS

Integrated Ballistics Identification System (IBIS) an electronic database of fired bullets and cartridge casings, created by Forensic

Technology in Montreal, Canada, in 1992; now linked with the similar FBI database, Drugfire, through the National Integrated Ballistics Information Network (NIBIN)

Kastle-Meyer test a modern test for identifying blood that uses phenolphthalein, a substance that turns bright pink when hemoglobin is present

lands the raised ridges in the rifling of a gun barrel or on a bullet; the lands alternate with grooves, or depressed areas

larynx an organ in the throat containing the vocal cords; also called the voicebox

latent prints fingerprints that become visible only when exposed to certain chemicals or special types of light. *Compare with* IMPRESSED PRINTS; PATENT PRINTS

lie detector any machine that is claimed to show when a person is lying; usually an informal name for the polygraph. *See* POLYGRAPH

livor mortis purplish patches that appear on the skin on the lower part of a body (that is, the part nearest the ground), beginning about half an hour after death, caused by gravity pulling red blood cells downward after the heart stops pumping blood; also called lividity

loop a category of fingerprint in which the ridges turn back on themselves. *Compare with* ARCH; WHORL

Luminol a spray that makes bloodstains exposed to it visible under ultraviolet light

maggot the wormlike young form, or larva, of a fly, often found infesting meat or dead bodies exposed to air

Marsh test a sensitive test for arsenic, developed by British chemist James Marsh in 1836

mass spectrometry a technique, usually used with gas chromatography, that bombards a gas with electrons in order to determine what chemicals are present in a mixture and in what proportions

medical examiner a physician authorized by a police department or other government agency to determine the cause of suspicious deaths. *Compare with* CORONER

medical jurisprudence a 19th-century name for what is now called forensic medicine

mitochondria small bodies within a cell that help the cell use energy; they contain DNA that is inherited from an organism's female parent

Mongoloid one of three main racial types; it refers to humans primarily from Asia or Oceania but also includes Native Americans. *Compare with* CAUCASOID; NEGROID

mutation a change in the sequence of bases in a gene; it may be inherited or produced by a factor in the environment, such as radiation

National DNA Index System (NDIS) a national electronic database of DNA profiles from convicted criminals, established by the FBI in 1998. *See also* COMBINED DNA INDEX SYSTEM

National Integrated Ballistics Information Network (NIBIN) a computer program that lets the Drugfire (U.S.) and IBIS (Canadian) forensic ballistics databases exchange information

Negroid one of three main racial types; it refers to humans primarily of African descent. *Compare with* CAUCASOID; MONGOLOID

nicotine a poisonous alkaloid found in tobacco plants

nucleus a central body in most types of cells; it contains DNA

patent prints fingerprints that are visible without any special treatment. *Compare with* IMPRESSED PRINTS; LATENT PRINTS

paternity suit a lawsuit in which a woman claims that a certain man is the father of her child and the man denies it; DNA profiling can settle such suits

pathology the study of diseased or injured tissue

pelvis the ring of bones at the lower end of the trunk (the hips), to which the legs attach

periphery camera a camera designed to photograph the whole curved surface of a bullet at once

phenolphthalein a chemical that turns bright pink when hemoglobin is present; used in a test for the presence of blood

physical anthropology the study of physical differences between human beings

pitch a property of sound related to frequency; the higher the frequency, the higher the pitch

plasma the liquid part of the blood, including both serum and substances that make the blood clot. *Compare with* SERUM

plastic prints *See* IMPRESSED PRINTS

polygraph a machine, invented by John Larson and Leonarde Keeler in the 1920s, that is supposed to be able to detect lying by measuring changes in blood pressure, heartbeat rate (pulse), breathing, and galvanic skin response; popularly called the lie detector

polymerase chain reaction (PCR) a technique, invented by Kary Mullis in 1983, that rapidly and repeatedly duplicates small samples of DNA

poroscopy a technique of identification, developed by Edmond Locard in the early 20th century, that counts the pores within fingerprints

precipitate a solid substance produced from a liquid (solution) by a chemical or physical change

precipitin See ANTIBODY

precipitin test See BORDET TEST

protein one of a large family of chemicals that does most of the work in cells

pubic symphyses the parts of the two hip bones that meet in the front of the pelvis; forensic anthropologists use changes in these bones to determine a body's age

red blood cells cells in the blood that contain hemoglobin and carry oxygen to the tissues

resonators cavities of the mouth, nose, and throat, the parts of the vocal system that shape and amplify sound waves produced by the vocal cords. *Compare with* ARTICULATORS

respiration breathing

Rh factor a blood antigen discovered first in rhesus monkeys but also present in humans; it was identified by Karl Landsteiner and Alexander S. Weiner in 1940

ridge minutiae tiny variations in fingerprint ridges, such as breaks or connections with other ridges; Francis Galton used these features to distinguish between similar fingerprints

rifling spiral grooves carved into a gun barrel to make a bullet spin in flight, thereby increasing the distance the bullet can fly and the accuracy of its aim

serology the study of body fluids, including blood, semen, saliva, and tears

serum the liquid part of the blood, after removal of substances that make blood clot. *Compare with* PLASMA

short tandem repeats short segments of DNA examined in DNA profiling tests; they replaced hypervariable regions in such tests in 1994

skull-face superposition a technique for identification in which the video image of a living face is placed over the image of a skull for comparison

sodium citrate a chemical that preserves blood; used alone, it preserves blood for about 10 days, but it can keep the blood fresh for a longer period if the blood is also refrigerated

soft palate the back part of the roof of the mouth, containing muscle but no bone

sound spectrograph a machine that produces a graphic representation of the variation in frequencies of sound waves over time; it can be used to produce such representations (spectrograms) for identification of voices

spectrogram the graph produced by a sound spectrograph, typically showing the frequencies within a 2.5-second stretch of spoken sound

stature the physical height of a person

stress physical and mental tension or strain caused by unpleasant conditions or events

striations marks on a bullet produced by rifling and imperfections in the barrel of the gun that fired it

sutures the lines where the bones of the skull meet

toxicology the study of poisons, including drugs (illegal or legal) and chemicals in the environment that affect human health

trace evidence tiny pieces of physical evidence, such as dust, hairs, and fibers

trait an inherited feature or characteristic of an organism

transfusion transfer of blood from one person or animal to another

vertebrae the individual bones that make up the spine, or backbone

Visual Speech term used by Melville Bell for his system of graphic representations of spoken sounds, developed in 1867

vocal cords bands of muscle tissue within the larynx (voicebox) that vibrate to make spoken sounds

voice stress test a test that claims to detect lying by changes in the voice

voiceprint a term coined by Lawrence G. Kersta for sound spectrograms used for voice identification

white arsenic arsenic oxide, a white powder used for many purposes, including poisoning

whorl a category of fingerprint pattern with ridges that turn through at least one complete circle. *Compare with* ARCH; LOOP

FURTHER RESOURCES

Books

Benecke, Mark. *Murderous Methods: Using Forensic Science to Solve Lethal Crimes*. New York: Columbia University Press, 2005.
German forensic scientist analyzes famous crimes such as the 1930s Lindbergh kidnapping case.

Evans, Colin. *The Casebook of Forensic Detection: How Science Solved 100 of the World's Most Baffling Crimes*. New York: Wiley, 1996.
Short descriptions of famous cases, grouped by forensic science specialty (toxicology, ballistics, trace evidence, and so on).

———. *Murder 2: The Second Casebook of Forensic Detection*. Hoboken, N.J.: Wiley, 2004.
Short chapters cover famous cases, forensic science specialties, and pioneers in the field.

Fridell, Ron. *Solving Crimes: Pioneers of Forensic Science*. New York: Franklin Watts, 2000.
For young adults. Profiles Alphonse Bertillon, Edward Henry, Karl Landsteiner, Edmond Locard, Clyde Snow, and Alec Jeffreys.

Genge, N. E. *The Forensic Casebook: The Science of Crime Scene Investigation*. New York: Ballantine Books, 2002.
Describes the work of various types of modern forensic scientists at the scenes of crimes and in the laboratory.

Petraco, Nicholas. *Illustrated Guide to Crime Scene Investigation*. Boca Raton, Fla.: CRC, 2005.
Guide to the techniques of processing a crime scene contains numerous photographs and diagrams.

Platt, Richard. *Forensics*. Boston: Kingfisher, 2005.
For young adults. Explains how detectives use various kinds of science to solve crimes.

Stewart, Gail B. *Forensics*. San Diego: Lucent Books, 2005.
For young adults. Describes the science and technology of criminal investigation.

Trimm, Harold. *Forensics the Easy Way.* Woodbury, N.Y.: Barrons, 2005.
    Introduction to forensic science for criminology students discusses such sub-
    jects as firearm analysis, fingerprints, and DNA evidence.
Wilson, Colin, and Damon Wilson. *Written in Blood: A History of Forensic
    Detection.* New York: Carroll & Graf reissue, 2003.
    Extensive history of forensic science, divided by specialty.
Yeatts, Tabatha. *Forensics: Solving the Crime.* Minneapolis: Oliver Press,
    2001.
    For young adults. Describes the careers of seven pioneers of forensic science.

Internet Resources

Carpenter's Forensic Science Resources. Tennesee Criminal Law. Available
    online. URL: http://www.tncrimlaw.com/forensic. Accessed on January
    7, 2006.
    Extensive links divided by forensic science type, including criminalistics and
    trace evidence, forensic anthropology, forensic entomology, and forensic
    exhibits and images.
Crime and Clues: The Art and Science of Criminal Investigation. Daryl
    W. Clemens. Available online. URL: http://www.crimeandclues.com.
    Accessed on January 7, 2006.
    Articles by various authors on aspects of crime scene investigation, death
    investigation, fingerprint evidence, physical evidence, and other types of evi-
    dence.
Federal Bureau of Investigation Kids' Page. Federal Bureau of Investigation.
    Available online. URL: http://www.fbi.gov/fbikids.htm. Accessed on
    January 7, 2006.
    Material for 6th–12th graders includes history of the FBI, a day in the life of
    an FBI agent, how the FBI investigates, an FBI adventure, and an agent chal-
    lenge. Site also provides stories of famous past FBI cases.
Forensic Fact Files. National Institute of Forensic Science (Australia).
    Available online. URL: http://www.nifs.com.au/factfiles/topics.asp.
    Accessed on September 24, 2005.
    Discusses a variety of forensic science fields, including anthropology, finger-
    prints, and serology, from the viewpoint of students and teachers. Describes
    what each field is, how it is used, famous cases, and activities.
Forensics and Investigation. Court TV Crime Library. Available online.
    URL: http://www.crimelibrary.com/criminal_mind/forensics. Accessed on
    September 22, 2005.
    Groups of essays by Katherine Ramsland describe forensic science fields,
    famous cases, and leading forensic scientists.

Forensic Science. ThinkQuest. Available online. URL: http://library.think-quest.org/04oct/00206/index1.htm. Accessed on January 7, 2006.
> For students and teachers. Contains sections on crime scene, autopsy, identity, evidence, suspects, weapons, and trickery. Resources include a glossary, experiments, lesson plans, and case studies. An interactive section supplies interviews, quizzes, and science experiments.

Forensic Science Central. Stephanie Rankin. Available online. URL: http://www.forensicsciencecentral.tk. Accessed on January 7, 2006.
> Articles on numerous forensic science topics, aimed at students and nonprofessionals.

Forensic Science Web Pages. Available online. URL: http://home.earthlink.net/~thekeither/Forensic/forsone.htm. Accessed on January 7, 2006.
> Topics covered on the site include firearms and toolmark identification, personal identification, and crime scene processing.

MegaLinks in Criminal Justice. T. O'Connor, Austin Peay State University. Available online. URL: http://www.apsu.edu/oconnor. Last updated January 3, 2006. Accessed on January 7, 2006.
> Provides links to topics including crime analysis, criminology, and policing, as well as extensive notes for classes on criminology, criminal investigation, and related subjects.

NCSTL Website/Database. National Clearinghouse for Science, Technology and the Law. Available online. URL: http://www.ncstl.org/search. Accessed on December 4, 2005.
> Searchable database covers subjects such as blood pattern analysis, crime scene investigation, and DNA. It provides listings of Web sites, reports, radio and television shows, books and more for each of these topics.

Science Fair Projects and Experiments: Forensic Science. Julian T. Rubin. Available online. URL: http://www.juliantrubin.com/forensicprojects.html. Accessed on January 7, 2006.
> Students' accounts of science fair projects on fingerprinting and other forensic science topics.

3D Crime Scene. Paul Breuninger. Available online. URL: http://www.forensic.to/webhome/paulb. Accessed on January 7, 2006.
> Includes three-dimensional diagrams of crime and crash scenes, bullet trajectories, bloodstain pattern analysis, forensic anthropology, cold cases, and more.

Virtual Exhibit on Forensic Science. Virtual Museum of Canada. Available online. URL: http://www.virtualmuseum.ca/Exhibitions/Myst/en. Accessed on January 8, 2006.
> Includes a database and time line of forensic science and an interactive game in which the participator uses forensic science skills to solve a murder.

Who Dunnit? Cyberbee.com. Available online. URL: http://www.cyberbee. com/whodunnit/crime.html. Accessed on September 22, 2005.
Interactive site for young people discusses fingerprinting, teeth impressions, powders, and more. It provides questions, skill-building assignments, and resources on each topic.
Young Forensic Scientists Forum. American Academy of Forensic Scientists. Available online. URL: http://www.aafs.org/yfsf. Accessed on January 7, 2006.
Site is aimed at students interested in forensic science or training to become forensic scientists. It includes a newsletter, essays by student forensic scientists, and a discussion of forensic science as a career.

Periodicals

Forensic Examiner
Published by the American College of Forensic Examiners
2750 East Sunshine Street
Springfield, MO 65804
Telephone: (800) 423-9737
Includes research articles, lectures, and descriptions of education courses

Forensic Science International
Published by Elsevier Inc.
360 Park Avenue South
New York, NY 10010
Telephone: (212) 989-5800
International journal devoted to applications of medicine and science in administration of justice Publishes research, reviews, and case reports in a variety of forensic science specialties

Journal of Criminal Law and Criminology
Published by Northwestern University School of Law
357 East Chicago Avenue
Chicago, IL 60611
Telephone: (312) 503-8547
Professional journal that provides a forum for dialogue and debate on current criminal law and criminology issues

Journal of Forensic Science
Published by the American Academy of Forensic Sciences
410 North 21st Street, Suite 203
Colorado Springs, CO 80904-2798
Telephone: (719) 636-1100
Covers established specialties including toxicology and physical anthropology, as well as emerging disciplines such as forensic sculpting and polygraph examination

Law Enforcement Technology
Published by Officer.com and Cygnus Business Media
1227 Mountainside Trace
Kennesaw, GA 30152
Telephone: (770) 427-5290
Monthly magazine for law enforcement managers that concentrates on emerging trends and technological advances being made in the field of law enforcement

Science and Justice
Published by the Forensic Science Society
18A Mount Parade
Harrogate, North Yorkshire HG1 1BX
United Kingdom
Telephone: (44 0) 1423-506-068
Quarterly journal for members

Societies and Organizations

American Academy of Forensic Sciences (http://www.aafs.org) 410 North 21st Street, Suite 203, Colorado Springs, CO 80904-2798. Telephone: (719) 636-1100.

Canadian Society of Forensic Science (http://www.csfs.ca) 3332 McCarthy Road, Ottawa, Ontario, Canada K1V 0W0. Telephone: (613) 738-0001.

Federal Bureau of Investigation (FBI) (http://www.fbi.gov) J. Edgar Hoover Building, 935 Pennsylvania Avenue NW, Washington, DC 20535-0001. Telephone: (202) 324-3000.

Forensic Science Society (http://www.forensic-science-society.org.uk) 18A Mount Parade, Harrogate, North Yorkshire HG1 1BX, United Kingdom. Telephone: (44 0) 1423-506-068.

International Association for Identification (http://www.theiai.org) 2535 Pilot Knob Road, Suite 117, Mendota Heights, MN 55120-1120. Telephone: (651) 681-8566.

INDEX